why me God?

by Robert N. Schaper

G/L
REGAL
BOOKS

A BIBLE
COMMENTARY
FOR LAYMEN

A Division of G/L Publications
Glendale California, U.S.A.

© Copyright 1974 by G/L Publications
All rights reserved
Printed in U.S.A.

Second Printing, 1974
Third Printing, 1977

Published by
Regal Books Division, G/L Publications
Glendale, California 91209, U.S.A.

Library of Congress Catalog Card No. 73-82763
ISBN 0-8307-0452-3

contents

A teaching and discussion guide for individual
or group study with this book is available
in a G/L Teaching Kit from your church supplier.

introduction

There is no lack of literature on the book of Job. Every generation since Gutenberg has had its array of titles on this great portion of Scripture. Even before Gutenberg the handwritten manuscripts were not without commentaries, sermons and theological discussions on the man from Uz. This abundance of material demands a reason for another book on Job, and there is one; hopefully, several.

There is need for a condensed and inexpensive resource for individual and group study of this important book of the Bible. The growth, both inside and outside of the church, of interest in the study of the Bible is a most welcome trend. Some portions of the Bible, for obvious reasons, have been thoroughly exposed to the interested student. Yet many people who attempt to take their Christian commitment quite seriously know little of the Old Testament, and even less of its more difficult sections.

It is the purpose of this book to discuss in orderly fashion the contents and leading ideas of the book of Job. It is to be hoped that this writing will be profitable and understandable reading in itself. It is more to be hoped that the reading will be preceded, interrupted and followed by a reading of the book of Job.

This is intended to be a "popular" book in that it is directed to the nonprofessional. The benefit of this work will come to the Christian who wants to know his Bible better and thereby know his Lord. There is no need to label the work as "practical"; that aspect of the book of Job is inescapable if we are honest with the material.

Though "all Scripture is inspired by God and profitable for doctrine" (2 Tim. 3:16), the development of our contemporary culture as expressed in its major philosophy, its art forms and its new life styles has made the book of Job exceptionally useful. Here is a book that strikes at the root problems and concerns of mankind. It forces on the reader an honest exploration of questions that are mystifying and conditions that are perplexing. Here is a book for everyone who has ever asked "Why?" for anyone who ever suffered, be the anguish mental, emotional or physical.

facing the issues

Let's start with a question: "Does life have a way of settling accounts?" Or we might ask this: "Do the good guys always come out on top?"

Have you, like many of us, watched the puzzling collapse of a good person? One I knew was young, brilliant, vital. He was well into a promising career, a dedicated and capable man. He was the father of a small family and the joy of his parents. We all hoped against hope that the surgery had been successful. Five years slipped by and then the dreaded growth reappeared, and after a few painful weeks, he died.

I remember walking out of the hospital and driving through a world that was going on as though nothing had happened. I rode through a kind of Skid Row and watched some of the derelicts shuffling along the sidewalk or sprawled in doorways. Middle-aged, some of them. A few were old men. They showed in their faces the marks of dissipation and despair, yet they were alive; and not far away a mortician was preparing a good, young, Christian man's body for burial. Where is God? Why?

Is there any question sharper or more acute than that? It has been asked in every generation because so much in every generation produces the question. Perhaps there is more to raise the question in the twentieth century than any other. Why does God allow the suffering and frustration in the world? If He is God, then He must have the power to stop it. If He is good, why doesn't He?

Archibald MacLeish has written a play that puts this book of Job in a contemporary setting. He called it *J.B.* and the whole point of the play is to penetrate this nagging question of why there is so much unrelieved suffering and death in the world. In the play the counterpart of Satan, who is called Nickles, comments: "If God is God He is not good; if God is good, He is not God." The playwright comments further on the problem:

"Millions and millions of mankind
Burned, crushed, broken, mutilated,
Slaughtered, and for what? For thinking!
For walking round the world in the wrong
Skin, the wrong-shaped noses, eyelids:
Sleeping in the wrong city . . ."*

I remember the stunned looks on the faces of the mother and father to whom the news had just been delivered. Their daughter, a lovely girl in her early

* From *J.B.* by Archibald MacLeish. New York: Samuel French, Inc. Copyright 1958 by Archibald MacLeish.

2

thirties, had some years before married a most admirable and dedicated man. After a try at business he had felt the call of God to missionary service. Together with his wife, he had completed Bible school training and been accepted for service in the South Pacific. God had given them a darling family of four children. Now the word had come. On a brief flight in a small plane to a nearby mission station trouble developed and the plane crashed. Their ten-year-old was the only survivor. All the rest, dead.

Ten thousand questions loomed behind the tears. What a tragic waste of limited personnel for such a great task! What a blow to faithful parents who had prayed and sacrificed and given up their children to the service of God! What is to be said? Who is at fault? Where is any evidence of wisdom or plan?

Then there seemed to be a possible way out. Further details of the story revealed that the surviving little boy was found by a very remote tribe of primitive people. Earlier attempts to open this tribe to friendly communication of the gospel had been unsuccessful. But since they were unconcerned over any threat to themselves from the boy, they took good care of him. When contact was finally made to rescue the boy, the fear and withdrawal of this tribe seemed to vanish. Instead, they requested that some Christians return and share their message with these people.

Was this the key to this sad event? Was this sacrifice the doorway to the entrance of the gospel to people who would otherwise not listen to it? I remember how quickly well-meaning Christians suggested this, nodding their heads knowingly as though the councils of the Eternal had been opened wide to them. Would that satisfy you? This father and mother smiled their appreciation for the comfort of friends, but what might you and I be thinking deep inside? I for one could easily think of all kinds of ways to get at a tribe of pagans without killing a whole family of missionaries.

Two great underlying problems are being raised by the events I have described, events which are duplicated in some fashion in the experience of every one of us. The simple, direct, straightforward, obvious difficulty is the problem of the bad things that happen to good people.

I presume we would agree that this does happen. We will see when we plunge into this fascinating book of Job that it is possible to deny that this happens. We could go at the whole matter of suffering and difficulty as clear evidence that the person involved is guilty of something or other that has a direct line relationship with the suffering and difficulty. But if we don't want to say this, then the problem is there: bad things do happen to good people, and the question is, why?

Job does say something about this age-old problem of why the righteous suffer. It would be impossible for the story of a sufferer like Job not to have some comment on that. Yet the book does not stop with this obvious problem. The necessity for an answer reveals the deeper problem, the real value and motivation of serving God. Does it pay to serve God? Is God fair in His dealings with mankind? What kind of faith does He want from us?

Specifically, what does it take to keep faith in God

4

as loving, just, sovereign and concerned when everything falls to pieces? What kind of insight is necessary to make sense out of life, or failing that, to make its lack of sense acceptable?

Perhaps the importance and helpfulness of the book of Job begins to impress you. It is going to push past the solutions that we are fed most of the time when we are instructed about life's problems.

How many times have we been told that the way to "get through" is to remember that there are others who have suffered or are suffering as we are, or, hopefully, even worse? "I wept because I had no shoes until I saw a man who had no feet." There is a simple wisdom and momentary comfort in that, but it means rather little when the one who says it to the barefoot person walks by in a new pair of boots.

My trouble is that whenever I am told to look for the man who has it as bad as I do or even worse, my head keeps turning and I usually see someone who is wonderfully better off than I am, and most of the time he doesn't really seem that much nicer or more worthy.

Neither does the book of Job suggest that the problem is one of our inner attitude, though this might prove of some relevance. The answer for Job is not just to think positively. It seems to me that the deeper one has to dip into the well of suffering, the more hollow and empty the advice to think positively becomes. Positive thinking works with minor crises. I guess Job could have applied it at first when he lost his oxen, and it might have carried him through the sheep and camels; but a positive attitude would have been a mockery after the loss of all his children and the sudden, horrible collapse of his health. How do you think positively about that?

Neither does the book try to avoid the involvement of God in the events and experiences of our lives. No one suggests that there is any comfort in letting life be a series of fortuitous, uncharted, unpredictable circumstances. Life is not a "tale told by an idiot, full of sound and fury signifying nothing." Merely to shrug our shoulders and mumble how that's the way the cookie crumbles is no answer at all.

This is not to say that Job is a book of answers. In the final analysis, the book will bring us to a confrontation with God. But that confrontation does not mean discovering a grand blueprint or plugging in to a master, monster computer that will flash answers when the proper buttons are punched. To face God is not to get answers, but to rephrase all our questions.

So there are two questions. The first is touched on the way to the second. The surface question is: Why does suffering come to good people? Yet this is secondary to the more basic question that acts as the compelling force for the entire book: Is it possible to trust God without being convinced that present benefit will result, or to trust even in the face of overwhelming trouble?

This particular book is especially pertinent in the last half of the twentieth century. Consider the impact of Freud and the realization of the psychic dimensions of human existence. Job moves in the deepest recesses of trauma and pain, brushes aside all convention and pretense and reaches into the kind of honesty and self-consciousness that psychotherapy is always looking for. This same mood prevails in the arts, which painfully reflect the restive spirit and disorganized condition of modern man. Existential philosophy and its counterpart in the crisis theology of Barth and those who followed him drink at the same fountain as the man of Uz who knew himself best in the moment of his encounter with God.

Regardless of the depth to which we are able to press, Job will speak to us. Our lives may seem reasonably uncomplicated, our brains untortured by problems of existence and eternity, yet at some point, sooner or later, we will find this book speaking to our need.

The wisdom of the ages is to discover truth and insight in advance of the crisis, and then to transform the wind of adversity into a friendly breeze that shoves our little ship unerringly toward the last, best haven. Job could help you do just that.

Don't think for a moment that it takes forty-two chapters to say what I have just said. All other kinds of ideas are presented as the dramatic story unfolds. It will be our privilege to look at these one by one.

2
a look at the whole book

AN OVERVIEW

For your first exercise with this book try to grasp its entire scope so that you can quickly feel at home in any part of it. You might leaf through it, scanning here and there just to see what's going on. Set yourself the goal of really knowing Job by the time you finish this study. There is no substitute for multiplied readings to give you proper familiarity with a volume.

Perhaps you would find it helpful to read a summary, a kind of overview of the book, and thus get a better idea about it. The major divisions of the book are relatively easy to determine.

Prologue/Job 1 and 2

This, along with the Epilogue and some few other verses, is the prose section of the book and describes the actual story that gives rise to the discussions of the Dialogue. Job, a wealthy patriarch of the unknown land of Uz (probably Edom), is a hero of great personal integrity and exemplary concern for the well-being of his fine family. He becomes the focus of interest at a heavenly assembly when God asks the Adversary (Satan) if, in his examination of the actions of mankind, he has considered Job. Satan protests that since Job is so prosperous, Job is getting a great deal out of his obedience. He predicts Job's downfall if providential protection is removed. The contest begins. Job's possessions and family are destroyed, yet Job clings to his trust in God. Satan then pushes the test to Job's health, and Job is smitten with a most loathsome disease. In spite of the urgings of his wife to "curse God and die," Job affirms his resignation to the will of God. He is then visited by three friends, Eliphaz, Zophar and Bildad.

Dialogue/Job 3—42:6

This major portion of the book begins with a lament by Job that seems a contradiction of the resigned figure of the Prologue. The friends who presumably came to comfort now become antagonists accusing Job mercilessly. As he answers each speaker in turn he steadfastly maintains his innocence. In the three series of statements and replies, the friends do not really advance in their arguments, but Job muses over various possibilities to explain his problems (Job 4—27). Chapter 28 is a most unexpected hymn on Wisdom inserted just before Job's final statement (Job 29—31). Then there appears a new character, Elihu, a younger man who has been listening to the entire discussion and now feels compelled to make his observations (Job 32—37). He tries to show the instructive and maturing quality of suffering, but Job does not reply. Instead we have the voice of God out of the whirlwind that challenges Job to answer numerous questions, all showing the power of God as evidenced in the natural creation (Job 38—42:6). Job is contrite and satisfied.

Epilogue/Job 42:7-17

The writing returns to prose. Job is now vindicated as God orders the friends to seek mercy through the intercession of Job. When Job mediates for them, God restores Job to his former greatness, doubles his possessions and children, and Job finally dies in old age, a happy and fulfilled man.

SOME IMPLICATIONS

The book of Job not only seeks to give some answers, it instructs us in how to ask the questions. In fact, it tells us what the questions really are. Let's review the practical implications.

1. The major thrust of the Dialogue is to show the inadequacy of the simple formula of retributive justice to explain *all* the circumstances of life. This is replaced by the suggestion that some who suffer are really saints, and that there is no answer to their problem but confidence in God just because God is God.

2. The story of Job and his final vindication is also an instruction in resignation to the will of God and a defense of the possibility of pure-hearted worship of God. The question posed is, "Does Job fear

God for nought?" The answer is yes, and Job proves it by clinging to God even when everythng is taken from him.

3. In the final analysis, Job and his righteousness fade before the majesty and holiness of God, who nonetheless accepts and restores Job. This is an amazing foreshadowing of justification by faith based on the unmerited favor of God. Job wonders how a man can really be just with God and finds the answer in God Himself, not his own goodness or understanding.

It is a thrilling experience to study this book and find the way in which the author gropes for the various things that would give new hope and courage in the midst of the problems Job faced. These are the very things offered to us in the gospel: favor for us before God in the person of Christ; hope for resurrection and ultimate justice and righteousness; access to the throne of God without fear or barrier. If Job could, with his limited revelation, cling to his trust in God, what should be our joy and confidence in the light of the Cross and the Empty Tomb?

3
prologue of Job

JOB, HIS PIETY AND PROSPERITY/JOB 1:1-5

As we now plunge into the book itself, a careful reading of the text is indispensable. Your own reactions and responses are of great importance.

Job's Piety

Job's greatness is first of all moral. He is "perfect and upright," a description that, to a Hebrew reader, would never imply sinlessness. He was blameless in that he responded properly to God, lived according to righteous principles and accepted full responsibility for his actions. His godliness had a positive and negative aspect. First he feared God. In the Old Testament, the fear of God was always the "beginning of wisdom" (Prov. 1:7). It was the essence of the first table of the Law. "Thou shalt love the Lord," was never out of harmony with the "fear of the Lord," for this fear was an awareness of majesty, not a cowering, craven subjection. The negative, "turned away from evil," is an inevitable corollary, a "Thou shalt not," which follows the "Thou shalt." True piety does not deny the negatives, but it does not begin with them or major in them either.

Job's Prosperity

His family Everything about this man is ideal. Job's family is exemplary. He has seven sons and three daughters. This sounds like just the right number for a great man's household. They exhibit amazing harmony and love. The daughters' sharing in the family activity was unusual, since women were not normally given this privilege. Feasting in the various homes was probably an annual celebration, perhaps at the New Year. Although Job was not included in these events, he did not resent it. He knew that his children were not above weakness and imperfections so he offered sacrifices for them. These are exceptionally mature parental attitudes. Note that Job is presented in ideal terms, a kind of representative man, one who exemplifies virtues that all of us would like to have. He is Everyman at his best, especially in relation to his family.

Job's possessions An idealized list of possessions establishes Job as the greatest man of his country. Note the figures: 7,000, 3,000, 500 and 500. These have the symbolic significance of completion. The value of Job's property compares with that of a typical, semi-nomadic chieftain. As great as his possessions were, they did not serve to corrupt him. In his final defense Job even protests that his wealth was a constant source of blessing to the poor (Job 31:15-22).

The Old Testament does teach that the blessing of God is best demonstrated in material wealth and personal prosperity. However, the ideal for the Christian is not Abraham, David or Job. This Old Testament principle must always be refined by New Testament understanding. Jesus took His place with the poor. None of the disciples were men of affluence or prestige.

This is not to teach a renunciation of wealth, as in monasticism, but it does put us on our guard as to the deceitfulness of riches and the subtlety of covetousness.

THE FIRST TEST/JOB 1:6-22
The Scene
We are now taken to the royal court of heaven. The "sons of God," angelic beings, are brought in array before God. One is cast in the role of an adversary. He is called *The Satan,* a title meaning accuser (Zech. 3:2). This angelic being is interesting. Although it would seem he is not part of the angelic host, yet it is not inappropriate for him to be in the heavenly court. And although he is not described as essentially evil, his office seems to be one of ferreting out evil in mankind and drawing attention to it. He is very much like a secret policeman, probing for defections and reporting his findings. He becomes an "agent provocateur" when he finds that Job is a righteous man, and impugns Job's motives, even to the point of suggesting a means for his downfall. This malicious attitude is in line with the eventual development of what the Bible teaches about Satan as "the accuser of the brethren." The strict limits on his

power to touch God's people foreshadow New Testament teaching of divine restraint over the powers of evil.

Satan throws down the challenge: "Job has good reason to obey God," he says, "because obeying God pays so handsomely. Take away the dividends, and Job's obedience will turn to cursing." So God agrees to the destruction of Job's property and family.

This difficult sequence must be understood in context. It is a statement about the mystery of evil but certainly not an explanation of it. It accommodates itself to our human understanding, but does not solve the riddles. What about the children of Job and their right to life? Is God establishing a pattern here? Should the Christian expect to lose his wealth as soon as he acquires it? It hardly seems necessary for an omnipotent, omniscient God to be engaged in what is essentially just a wager, a contest. The story suggests once more the complexity of cosmic evil, never really understood by man, just as it was never really understood by Job. In the light of the rest of Scripture, however, we need not assume that God puts his servants to such difficult tests whenever Satan suggests that their faith is weak.

The Attack

Now the drama unfolds. In melodramatic fashion, messengers arrive telling Job of the annihilation of his possessions and family. Notice the combination of natural and human forces. Possessions are stolen by marauding bands but also destroyed by natural causes. His family is caught in a tornado, which we still describe for insurance purposes as "an act of

God." The agents behind these events are completely hidden. In one crushing, crashing moment Job is brought to poverty and grief. Prosperity had not destroyed his faith. What would adversity do?

The Result

Job's response is exemplary. "The Lord gave, the Lord hath taken away" (v. 21). This is resignation at its best.

A well-known prayer ascribed to many sources goes: "O God, give me grace to accept what cannot be changed; strength to change what can be changed; and wisdom to know the difference." In some situations, learning how to accept the inevitable is a difficult but necessary discipline. But resignation is not always the proper response to adversity. Sometimes refusal to accept the unacceptable is one of our greatest human capabilities. In the Muslim world and in India millions have settled with disease, wretchedness and poverty as the will of Allah or some irrevocable expression of fate. The Hebrew-Christian tradition rejects this kind of resignation because it gives an incomplete view of God.

To believe in the fall of man and the radical nature of evil is to reject things as they are in favor of things as they can be and ought to be.

Yet Job's reaction to his loss is amazing and instructive. After the Sabeans, the lightning, the Chaldeans and the great wind have struck, Job says, "The Lord has taken away. Blessed be the name of the Lord"[*] (v. 21). Beyond nature, beyond wicked men,

---

[*] The superior numbers with Scripture quotations throughout this book refer to Bible translations listed on "For Further Reading" page.

Job saw God. Clinging to God was the only way he could bring one stick of sense into the mystery of life.

THE SECOND TEST/JOB 2:1-10
The Scene
Once again the court of heaven is described. The Satan returns and grudgingly admits defeat, but insists that he has not finished making his point. "Skin for skin" (v. 4) is a strange statement, fortunately explained in the next phrase, "All that a man has he will give for his life'" (v. 4). "Job still has his health," argues the accuser, "and a man can stand the loss of anything but that. Touch his flesh and he will curse God." Without hesitation God now allows this last bitter attack on Job's integrity. Heaven then waits to see whether a man will worship God and trust Him even after everything has been taken from him.

The Sickness
Now Job received the final blow. It is not clear whether he went to the ash-heap as a symbol of mourning or whether he was cast out there by his apprehensive fellow-citizens. Probably it was the latter. Miserable and rejected, Job sat outside the village in the dump where animal dung and other refuse was burned.

We do not know what his sickness really was. The term in Job comes from a root word similar to the word used in Deuteronomy 28:35 which seems to refer to elephantiasis, a common disease in Egypt. Many have suggested, therefore, that Job had that disease. However, the word used in Job generally implies fever, inflammation and the like. Nothing else in the book of Job suggests the symptoms normally appearing with elephantiasis. In fact, Job seems to be "wasting away," hardly an accurate term for describing elephantiasis. There are many different kinds of skin infection in the Near East: "Baghdad Button," or "Jericho Rose," and "Oriental Sore." Perhaps, like Paul's thorn in the flesh, it is better that the specific illness be unknown. To add to his misery, Job probably brought on secondary infection by scraping himself.

There was more to this ordeal than just the physical symptoms, horrible as they were. Such an illness brought a clouding of the mind and a weakening of resolve and insight. It took almost superhuman effort for Job to retain any degree of composure. This was especially true when we consider the actions of his wife. She appears only once in the whole book. Although not taken along with Job's children, she gave Job a more severe test than he perhaps would have faced if she had been taken from him. Up to this point the glimpses of the family have not suggested that she was a constant problem. Yet the calamities coming upon her family were more than she could bear. She probably assumed that death was imminent for Job and that honesty demanded a vent for her feelings. Thus it is not surprising that early commentators regarded her as a subtle part of Satan's plot.

Success

In spite of terrible illness and the encouragements of his wife to bitterness, Job remained faithful. His remonstrance of his wife placed her with the "foolish women" (v. 10). Foolishness in the Bible always has a religious connotation. The fool says there is no God (Psalm 14:1). Jesus warns of calling another a fool. To be foolish is to lack spiritual discernment. Job sees that lack in his wife's attitude and tells her so. Again he resigns himself to God's will.

Job's wife encouraged him to do the very thing that the Satan had predicted he would do, blaspheme God. He refused, and "sinned not with his lips." The Old Testament idea of sin still centered on the outward act rather than the inner motivation and attitude. So Job emerged successfully from this ordeal.

THE COMFORTERS/JOB 2:11-13

The setting for the poetic dialogue is created by the arrival of "Job's comforters," those three famous men who are now associated with any project that discourages when it is supposed to encourage. A fourth man, Elihu, is not introduced, even though he gives his word as well (Job 32—37). Most of what is said about these men is conjecture. Their names are not discernibly symbolic. If their names ever did mean anything significant to the story, that meaning has been lost. Even their homelands are obscure. Eliphaz is from Teman, often placed near Petra in Nabatean territory. Bildad was descended from Shuah, a brother of Midian and the uncle of Sheba and Dedan, mentioned in Genesis 25:3. This would also denote a southerly location. Zophar was from Naamah, a town in the Judean foothills, mentioned in Joshua 15:41. Its exact location is unknown.

There is no indication how they knew of Job's condition and arranged to meet. Their initial experience with Job is commendable. They gave traditional evidence of their grief by weeping audibly, tearing their robes and sprinkling dust on themselves. Then they sat down and remained silent, awaiting the first words of the sad sufferer. They were properly shocked at the terrible condition of Job, barely recognizing him in his disfigured and despondent condition.

I mention these things because it is not going to go well with these men and we should give them all due credit whenever possible. They did at least come to Job. How many of our visits to the sick have been matters of good intention only? Jesus said, "I was sick and you visited me"[1] (Matt. 25:36).

They were also able to maintain compassionate silence. I must confess that I see symbolism again in this description of seven days seated on the ground without conversing. Seven hours of silence would seem an amazing discipline to me, and by the third day I would certainly reason that I would come back when Job wanted to talk! But don't miss in this circumstance the beautiful example of patient silence in the presence of suffering. There will be in the rest of the story such flagrant violation of this principle that we need to recognize and acknowledge it now. Most of the time, the best thing a friend can do in a crisis is just to be there. The words and advice may or may not be adequate, but the presence is healing.

This original strength of these comforters soon proves temporary in the heat of discussion. We will look at each and his contribution, but we can say in advance that they sinned most against Job by not accepting him, by not taking him seriously enough, by

21

being more concerned about the correctness of their doctrine than the need and condition of their friend. For any of us who seek to be counselors, this is the lesson that must be relearned with every encounter. Nothing can substitute for loving acceptance. This revelation need not destroy truth or pervert doctrine, but it will keep us human, and that counts for something.

4

a surprising lament

As we enter the lengthy poetic dialogue of our book, I want to encourage you to read this poetry with openness to its dramatic and emotional force. C. S. Lewis, in his book *Reflections on the Psalms,* has commented on the fortunate parallel structure of Hebrew poetry. Lewis observes that this parallelism not only elaborates ideas, but it also is very translatable.

So read this lament in Job 3 as poetry, and allow its power to sweep you along. The only passage in Scripture that compares with Job 3 is Jeremiah 20:7-18. Even that passage, especially verses 14-18, may be a reflection of the feelings described here in Job 3.

This chapter is divided into three stanzas or divisions. Verses 1-10 tell of a curse upon the day of Job's birth; verses 11-19, his desire for rest in the shadows of Sheol; and verses 20-26, his question of the purposes of God in his sore trials.

SURPRISE THAT THERE IS A LAMENT

If you were reading this book for the first time you would be shocked at this outburst from Job. Up to this point his only response to his troubles has been the calmest resignation. When Job lost his family and possessions, he said nothing. After his health was blasted, he calmed his distraught wife. But now this has changed. The friends have compassionately remained in shocked silence, politely awaiting the first response from the sufferer. His cry of anguish and confusion, when it finally comes, is almost a relief to us, because it virtually puts Job back into the human race. This lament is a masterpiece for helping us understand something of the dark night of the soul. In fact, it is that seeming total blackness that so surprises us.

We have all encountered people who have met tragedy, perhaps great tragedy. If they have lived into middle age and had a reasonably good life up until then, the person with a philosophic attitude usually tries to make the best of it. He will usually reminisce and call to mind the happy days, the children, the place of prestige and significance and conclude that all in all, it was better to have lived than not to have lived. Not so with Job. He looks at his condition, his losses, and wails his misery.

Is this a clue to the fact that something deeper than we imagine is happening? We are facing the results of a seven-day silence. Does the twinge of despair come because suspicions have been creeping in? Is Job losing his grip on God? More probably it begins to appear that God has lost his grip on Job. This seems to be the real sense of the last verses

(25,26) of this chapter. Job mourns that the thing which he feared has come upon him. He is not at ease, he has no rest. This could refer to his illness, but it more probably speaks of an apprehension about life itself, and all that God is supposed to be doing. What more drastic and disquieting fear could come to a man of faith than to face the possibility that all his attitudes and actions may have been meaningless? Yet how can faith ever come to its radiant fulness unless it is pressed to despair?

The silence of the comforters was one of respect and compassion. Yet their responses indicate their growing conviction that Job had sinned against God. Job knew this would be their conclusion. It seemed the only logical one. Yet deep within he refused to accept that and the resulting confusion plunged him into despair. Nothing made sense. The only escape was the shadow of extinction by death. Perhaps the context will make his lament more understandable, though still surprising.

THE SURPRISE OF WHAT IS LEFT OUT

Another important aspect of this lament is what it does not include. The very nature of the material would make us look for some items that do not appear. When we finish reading the chapter, we breathe a sigh of relief. Job has not gone as far as we were afraid he might. We remember that the Satan had predicted that Job's losses would bring him to the place of cursing God. When Job keeps pressing his question, "Why?" and curses the day he was born and the night he was conceived, we know he is a breath away from lifting his fist to heaven and throwing his curse at God. But he doesn't—although he does stop blessing God.

He still must keep some hold on God, but he must somehow ventilate his grief. This well-recognized therapy has merit even for the Christian. Job had shown his great sorrow in appropriate ways, but the final magnitude of his calamity evoked this Niagara of anguish in which he calls for death, questions the divine purposes, envies the dead, weeps in the ashes, but does not curse God. His lament is not out of harmony with faith.

It is interesting to note the response of the Christian community to the death of Stephen, the first Christian martyr. Instead of some artificial kind of supposed Christian fortitude, we're told that "devout men buried Stephen and made loud lamentation over him"' (Acts 8:2). One of the great problems of Western culture has been our inability to express our feelings freely, whether they are joyous or sad.

Another surprising omission from Job's lament is any contemplation of suicide. Job wishes that he had never been born and curses the day he was born (vv. 1-10). He wishes death had already come, and longs for the quiet of Sheol, the dark abode of the dead (vv. 11-19). Why should God keep alive anyone who so devoutly desires the grave? (vv. 20-23). Yet the surprising thing is that there is no mention whatsoever of the possibility of suicide.

This third chapter is in every sense a soliloquy. It immediately reminds one of Hamlet. Hamlet seriously considers self-destruction and refuses from fear of its unknown results. Job longs for death and even welcomes the shadowy existence of Sheol that he feels it would bring. But he never gives a breath of consideration to suicide even as an option. Since God is the author of life, God is the only one who can withdraw life.

In the cultures surrounding Israel suicide was sometimes considered heroic. Never so among the Jews. It was a scandal when King Saul fell on his own sword (1 Sam. 31:4), even though he was escaping death at the hands of pagan enemies. Not that Job has no sense of fascination with death. The possibility intrigues him, but only as an escape from his confusion and anguish.

The twentieth century has witnessed an unusual philosophic development about death. There are those, especially playwrights and poets of the existential school, who make self-inflicted death the one great personal authentic act. They say that that is the only moment where one defies all other forces of the universe and becomes genuinely himself.

The Bible knows no such standard. Neither does it discuss suicide as a sin, though some have tried to interpret it so. "Thou shalt do no murder" can hardly refer to suicide. It is perhaps the essence of grace to consider a suicide as a person without proper human faculty for responsible action. God alone can judge to what extent a person is responsible for being in that condition.

THE SURPRISE OF WHAT JOB DOES SAY

We should follow our own advice and not take this poetic lament too literally. The poet is probing the depths of human anguish and what is said in such a lament does not deserve analysis as much as empathy. How helpful this really is! We can walk with a man in the very depths of sorrow and discover a certain dimension to his woe that makes our own deluge seem more bearable.

What does Job really say? His curses of life reflect the most desperate of human states. "I'm sorry I was conceived; I wish I hadn't been born." "I wish I had died early; I wish I were dead now." "Why does God extend my wretchedness?" Can you feel the isolation of this?

How deeply this speaks to the characteristic malaise of our time! Everywhere there is an aimlessness, a lack of purpose and direction. The politician laments the deterioration of life and offers himself as a modern Moses leading the captives to a promised land. While educators and sociologists struggle for a revived sense of meaning and new objectives for individual and corporate life, the lonely go on struggling hopelessly. Who has not experienced the problem of being locked into himself, unable to break free, unable to understand or really know another person?

Job's isolation was compounded by the loss of *all* his children. In a culture which looked on offspring as the only means of establishing permanency in the world, he had nothing left but questions and pain.

The deepest isolation of all is exposed by the psalmist and echoed by Jesus Christ in the fourth cry from the cross, "My God, My God, why hast thou forsaken me?" Job finds no refuge in God. His references to God in this third chapter are quite oblique. In verse 4 he calls on God to assist in blotting out the day of his birth. In verse 23 he mechanically comments on the futility of light for a person whom God has "hedged in." In neither instance is God a help or comfort to Job, but still he can't let go of God completely. In the time of anguish, the cry is, "My God." Even when forsaken it is, "My God." At the very time when God seems so remote comes the wistful admission that He is really still there.

Job's dilemma illustrates profound truth in the witticism, "Thank God, I'm an atheist." Although totally disillusioned Job still cannot deny his need for God. He sounds like the apostle Peter falling at Jesus' feet, grabbing Him desperately and saying, "Depart from me" (Luke 5:8).

In contrast, or perhaps as an alternative, to the life that Job curses, comes his wish for the quiet and rest of death. This naturally introduces the whole concept of the after-life in Old Testament thought. It is an extensive subject, beyond our survey now, but a few generalities will be helpful. The Bible has no place at all for the idea that death is extinction or the cessation of being. There is an underlying confidence that God continues to hold man's true being in His hand, even after death.

The condition of the dead was left to God and was not the subject of extensive speculation. The best that could be surmised was a kind of shadowy existence identified as Sheol. This was the beginning of the divine revelation given in the Scriptures about death and the world to come. It was true but incomplete. I have heard the illustration used that progressive revelation is like viewing a foggy landscape early in the morning when the details of the scene are obscure. Everything one can see is genuine, but only after the haze has gone and the light is brighter can things be put in perspective and be clearly delineated. In the same way, the understanding of life after death unfolds in the Old Testament.

The Hebrews at first believed that when the body died, the soul went to Sheol, the abode of departed spirits. Sheol was almost a neutral existence. All human distinctions of glory and rank were gone, as were all the suffering and deprivation that might have been on earth. Since the Hebrews believed the genuine unity of body and spirit was basic to authentic human existence, Sheol had to be a kind of half-life at best. Any distinctions brought about by living righteously or unrighteously on earth, were not detailed. That all the dead were there was especially humbling for the great ones of the world, whom death always brought low. The Jews assumed that the praise of God, possible for a complete human—body and spirit—was not equally possible for the person who, after death, was less than his true self.

Keeping all these ideas in mind is especially helpful in reading other statements in the Old Testament about life after death. (See Psalm 6:5; Psalm 39:13; Psalm 88:4-12.) Many Christians mistakenly assume that the Bible teaches an essentially Greek concept of the immortality of the soul. Therefore, it is extremely important to understand that the doctrine begun in the Old Testament points toward a physical resurrection. The truly Christian hope, rooted in Hebrew tradition, is that the total being, body and spirit, will eventually enjoy full existence in the presence of God. This does not mean that the spirit does not exist after death, but it does mean that whatever existence the spirit has after death it is less than the ultimate human existence which will come after resurrection.

The Jews had a high regard for the creation of man. They believed that when the spirit left the body it was not release from a prison but withdrawal into one. As Job peered through the mists he hoped for more than he knew. His hope has now been fulfilled and affirmed in the resurrection of Jesus Christ.

One other benefit of this teaching distinguished Israel from its neighbors. The Israelites were free from any oppressive presence of the dead in their ongoing life. They neither worshiped, sacrificed to, nor developed religious rituals for their ancestors. They respected them, sought to learn from them, and tried to emulate their virtues, but they were not in bondage to them.

It is difficult to know what Job really believed about his future life, but he did anticipate that it would be a relief from the suffering and difficulty he was facing. We must accept Job's despair and realize how terribly difficult life can become. Job is so confused and disillusioned that he does not appeal to God. He can only question God. Why has God not permitted Job the death that now seems so desirable? What is there to be gained in any more breath?

Are you a sufferer? Have you ever thrown up your hands at the stupidity and tragedy of life? Then the book of Job is for you.

PROBLEM PASSAGES

Although we are making no attempt to give a detailed study of each verse, it could prove helpful for me to point out possible difficulties of understanding which you might encounter in a simple reading of the text.

The "Leviathan" mentioned in verse 8 is a mythological figure. Meaning dragon, this word is also used for the crocodile in Job 41. A Leviathan was a well-known primeval dragon signifying chaos in Ugaritic mythology. Job is probably calling on "professionals" to do his cursing, much as Balak did with Balaam. (See Num. 22—24).

enter Eliphaz

THE SPEECHES OF JOB'S FRIENDS

The major portion of the book of Job is the interesting series of exchanges made by the three friends and the suffering patriarch. There are three statements by each of the comforters and a reply by Job to each. Several possibilities are open to us in order to gain insight into the progress of thought in the book. I have chosen to consider the friends separately, looking at each of their statements as well as at Job's answers. There is some discernible difference in the characterization of the friends, and there is also some progress of thought in Job as he deals with the arguments. The important thing is for us to get the impact of the major truths being set forth. The order is of secondary significance.

It might be to our benefit to think about the general content of the argument of Job's friends before looking at each one in particular. When all the words are added up the impact is fairly clear. These men are elaborating over and over again the basic orthodoxy that came to dominate Jewish thought. It has its roots in what is properly called ethical monotheism, which is a smooth way of saying that the Jewish belief in one God was expressed in obedience to a rigidly defined set of principles or laws.

When the whole idea of relationship to God is understood only in terms of justice, duty, and legality, God becomes further and further removed from the true heart and core of man's existence. There is no way such a relationship can be described as personal. And yet a personal relationship with God is man's most meaningful experience.

Why are we never at ease with a representative of authority that might not understand us at the level of our intentions or our desires? A police car is a most welcome sight if we are being robbed and need protection from a lawbreaker, but who of us does not respond nervously to the sight of the police car in our rear view mirror? We know that our driving is imperfect enough that a strict interpretation of the law would probably find us guilty of infraction at some point or other. We hope that proper allowances will be made, that our personal integrity will be recognized, and we feel it would be especially helpful if the policeman turned out to be a personal friend or a relative. This is a crude illustration of the difference between the covenant of law and the covenant of grace in the Bible.

Job's friends verbalized the orthodox line for the covenant of law. We will look at these items in more detail as we go through the various sections, but this is a summary of them:

1. It is the righteous man who receives God's blessing.

2. All evil is punished.

3. Trouble and sorrow are the result of sin.

4. Suffering for sin can have disciplinary value.

5. God does accept repentance.

6. God is completely and absolutely above man and the world.

7. Man, along with all creatures, is unworthy before God.

The Old Testament reinforces these ideas at many points. The prophets, such as Amos and Jeremiah, saw in the history of Israel the solemn reminder of divine retribution. Israel sinned against the covenant with Jehovah that bound her to keep God's law. When that happened, there could be but one result, divine judgment. Wise men, such as Solomon and other writers of wisdom, extolled the righteous man and commented on the inevitable results both of obedience and folly. "The Lord knows the way of the righteous, but the way of the wicked will perish.'" (Psalm 1:6).

This orthodoxy concealed a terrible flaw. It was the inability to recognize adequately the principle of grace upon which the covenant was founded. Why did God choose Israel? Was it because she was so great among the nations, or so exemplary? Not at all. The Exodus that formed the Israelites into a people was clearly an act of God's redeeming love. He had loved them first. Out of that gracious choice had come His covenant with them. To be sure this did not mean that they could do as they pleased. The conditions were clear:

"You have seen what I did to the Egyptians, and how I bore you on eagles' wings and brought you to myself. Now therefore, if you will obey my voice and keep my covenant, you shall be my own possession among all peoples; for all the earth is mine, and you shall be to me a kingdom of priests and a holy nation'" (Exod. 19:4-6).

Since the foundation of this covenant was grace, the love of God revealed in that should never become secondary in understanding God and the life of Israel. To allow retributive justice to become the only defining principle for self-understanding is to divorce religion from the true center of life. This was the problem of Jewish legalism. It came to full blossom in the Pharisaism of Jesus' day. It is the problem of Job's comforters. They desperately felt that their principles had to be right. Job objected that life didn't fit their principles.

Note this same tendency in the development of the New Covenant, which is another good name for Christianity. What age of Christian history has not been marked by the attempt to solidify the gospel into a neatly-arranged list of rules, with the accompanying tyranny of professionals who have carefully defined the rules for their own advantage?

The constant heresy in the Christian era, as well as in Old Testament history, has been that man is acceptable to God only on the basis of his good works. In other words, whatever a man does determines his acceptability or non-acceptability with God. The logical result of this view is that lack of trouble indicates

God's response to right behavior and trouble indicates God's response to wrong behavior.

By the time we finish this book, the great problem with that view—and the solution of the problem —should become clear. We will repeat it because the book of Job repeats it. The speeches of the three friends will be a triple salvo from the same gun.

THE SPEECHES OF ELIPHAZ/JOB 4; 5; 15; 22

Eliphaz' First Speech/Job 4 and 5

Eliphaz is probably the most attractive of the friends. He is the first speaker in each sequence and he seems to be the most sophisticated and learned. Probably the oldest of the three, he identifies himself with the experienced wise (Job 15:9,10). You may feel that he is more considerate of Job than the others, although it is shocking how cutting and cruel each of these "comforters" can become.

The origin of the name Eliphaz seems to be Edomite. It means "God crushes," but this does not have any clear significance in the narrative.

Now let's look at this first speech in some detail. We shall try to distinguish the major subject areas of these speeches.

Job 4:1-11 Eliphaz on God's Justice First, Eliphaz states his basic theory about the justice of God as it relates to Job's condition. He begins politely enough (v. 2), but this civility soon fades in his zeal for righteousness and it really never appears again. So much for gracious formalities. I feel a real sting to his words in verses 5,6. "Job, you were great as an instructor, but you can't take your own teaching!" Verse 6 seems to imply a confidence that everything will be all right for Job, although this is certainly insensitive to Job's loss of his children.

Verse 8 is a good summary of Eliphaz' smug position, "As I have seen, those who plow iniquity and sow trouble reap the same."[2] I have often heard messages on that text that dramatically and dogmatically proclaim against the evils of alcohol—a rather restricted use of the text, to be sure. Yet the same sentiment is found in Galatians 6:7, "Whatever a man sows, this he will also reap.'"[3] But a closer look reveals an amazing difference in the applications of Eliphaz and Paul. Eliphaz insists that a present harvest of trouble and sorrow is proof of evil seeds. Paul looks for harvest in God's final day when the true results of faith and love will most certainly be reaped. Paul is encouraging the man of faith; Eliphaz is discouraging any person who suffers now.

Job 4:12—5:7   The Message of Eliphaz' Vision
Now we have the only appeal in the book to a mystical religious experience. The description is fascinating (vv. 12-16). Yet what a strange message issues from this presumed supernatural revelation. How threatening when subjective religious experience is used to validate an idea! The later statement of God to Job's friends throws grave suspicion over this "vision" of Eliphaz: "You have not spoken of Me what is right, as My servant Job has'" (Job 42:8).

Eliphaz announces the message of the vision to be the complete separation of God and man, even of God and the highest of his creatures (Job 4:17-19). Not only is God high above us (transcendence) but we are unworthy just because we are creatures. The implication is that God is not and cannot be involved with us and that He really doesn't care! William James called this the "stagnant felicity of the Absolute." It is the complete opposite of the God of the Incarnation in Jesus Christ. This further demonstrates the peril of a theological dogmatism that seems formally correct but is personally and experientially withering and cold. What a marvelous comfort the idea of God's exaltation and man's creaturely unworthiness must have been to a man with boils sitting on an ash-heap!

Job 5:7 illustrates an important principle. "For man is born for trouble, as sparks fly upward."[1] Whenever we talk about man we may or may not be talking about "a man." The ability to prevent the general from overwhelming the particular is the key to our understanding of this verse and others like it. In the final analysis, life is not what is happening to "the nation," or "the race," or "our generation," except in the way it is happening to you and to me.

Job 5:8-27 Counsel for the Sufferer Eliphaz turns, with no concern for his own inconsistency, from an unmoved and withdrawn God to one who carefully orders the processes of justice among men. The key verse is 5:17, very similar to Proverbs 3:11. The only problem is that God is not chastening or disciplining Job, as we know from the Prologue; therefore, this marvelous truth of divine discipline is totally misapplied.

Note the tragic humor in 5:27: "Lo, this we have searched out; it is true. Hear, and know it for your good."[2]

Using a royal plural and purporting to speak for a

whole class of scholars and sages, Eliphaz is honest, but wrong. Even if he were right, he is so forbidding in his argument that he repulses most just when he claims to be winning most. God spare us from this kind of doctrinal victories!

Eliphaz' Second Speech/Job 15

The second speech of Eliphaz reflects the appropriate irritation he feels over Job's answers to him and his friends. The comforters are evidently not getting anywhere with this rebel, and perhaps sterner remonstrance is necessary. They are more convinced than ever that Job's adversity is the deserved retribution for his sin. And although admission of sin and repentance might work, they are wondering if Job isn't already beyond hope. So Eliphaz varies his statement but not his theme.

Job 15:1-16 Rebuke for Sin and Disobedience Eliphaz mocks Job for claiming to be one of the wise men. In verse 2 he as much as says Job is full of hot air (an understandable metaphor). But Eliphaz reveals his deep alarm in verse 4: "Indeed, you do away with reverence, and hinder meditation before God."[1] Here is the rigid traditionalist's fanatic fear of the non-conformist. Job doesn't fit the pattern, and the only conclusion must be that he is a threat to religion. Moffatt translates this verse: "You undermine religion with your threatening of God."

Job 15:7-16 Job's Presumption Eliphaz turns to a most familiar approach in religious debate. He attacks Job's attitude rather than his argument. "Job, who do you think you are? Don't these friends know anything? What about all the gray-heads who agree with us? Besides, you're all stirred up about this and speaking irrationally." Eliphaz then repeats his earlier statement that since God is so far removed from man at his best, how can a man at his worst, like Job, hope to find favor? (vv. 14-16).

Job 15:17-35 The Fate of the Wicked With accomplished poetic imagery Eliphaz describes the sad fate of the wicked man. In a heartless way it sounds just like what has happened to Job, so the conclusion should be obvious.

Eliphaz' Third Speech/Job 22

This is the third and final statement of Eliphaz. It is more cutting than the second. No longer is he discussing the general fate of the wicked, but the heinous sin of Job. Pity has fled with discernment in the wild rush to maintain a dogma.

Job 22:1-5 Job's Suffering as Evidence of His Sin Now Eliphaz pulls out all the stops: "Is not your wickedness great, and your iniquities without end?"[1] (v. 5).

Since it is no particular gain or loss to God for Job to be righteous, then Job's suffering has to be the result of his wickedness.

Job 22:6-11 A Catalog of Job's Sins Although Job specifically denies anything remotely resembling these actions in his final defense (Job 29—31), that does not prevent Eliphaz from making the accusation. It is almost a shouting contest.

Job 22:12-20 Job's Sin of Assuming Divine Indifference In a very clever play, Eliphaz picks up on Job's statements in 21:14-16. Job was there lamenting that the wicked presume on God's indifference and consider it useless to pray and yet they prosper. Eliphaz almost repeats Job's words but does so with irony, playing the part of the patient righteous man who knows God will bring destruction upon the wicked. He even mentions the "consuming fire" as a judgment of God, reminiscent of one of the ways in which Job's estate was destroyed (Job 1:16).

Job 22:21-30 Appeal for Repentance This is a passage of hope. It is amazing and challenging, that the Joban poet* lets the last words of Eliphaz be surprisingly warm and conciliatory. Though the poet's sympathies are obviously with the tragic hero, his portrayal of the friends is penetrating and imaginative. These are not bad men.

JOB'S RESPONSES TO ELIPHAZ/
JOB 6; 7; 17; 23; 24

We have already noted the difficulty in dealing with these speeches in their relationship to each other. Each speaker does not refer strictly to the arguments raised by the preceding speaker. He may be looking back a couple of spaces, or he may be continuing what he was saying previously almost without reference to the preceding speaker.

It is of benefit to consider Job's statements together. They probably form more of a progression in thought than the speeches of the friends. We lost some of the consecutive quality of this by considering separately the response to the friends, but this is not a serious loss.

---

* For an explanation of the term *Joban poet*, see Appendix A, under the heading, "Authorship and Date."

First Response to Eliphaz/Job 6 and 7

In one sense this first reply is a continuation of the soliloquy of chapter 3. Job is still ventilating the bitterness of his soul and desiring earnestly the nothingness of Sheol. Yet there is an added dimension to this grief. What he has now heard from a friendly counselor only plunges him further into the abyss.

Job 6:1-13   Job's Defense of His Bitterness   Job wants consideration for his "rash words." He is just completely inundated by grief and calamity, and his friends should know this (vv. 2-4). In fact, Job desires death so that he will remain faithful to God. He has made it so far (v. 10), but he knows he cannot hold out this well much longer, and things are already slipping away from him (vv. 11-13).

Job 6:14-30   Disappointment in His Friends   Job contends that there is a theological problem in a lack of kindness, and that such a lack is forsaking "true religion." He then proceeds to a vivid comparison of his friends to a desert wadi, the equivalent of our arroyos of the American West. Spring rains bring a rushing stream which fortunately soon dries up. He even accuses them of fear in seeing his calamity (v. 21). Are they afraid to get too close or seem too sympathetic? Orthodoxy has always had trouble knowing how to relate to those it condemns, even though Jesus seemed unperturbed by association with publicans and harlots.

Job 7:1-21   Renewed Complaint   I do not find even the statements of chapter 3 any more moving or pitiable than this chapter. Job faces the confusion of his deep longing for an end to this suffering and misery coupled with his fear of nothingness and natural desire for life. He looks at his condition, and sees no hope (vv. 1-11). God will not leave him alone, even disturbing his sleep with terrifying dreams. Then we have a parody on Psalm 8, beginning at verse 17: "What is man that Thou dost magnify him, and that Thou art concerned about him, that Thou dost examine him every morning, and try him every moment?" The ultimate in Job's boldness is in verse 20: "Have I sinned? What have I done to Thee?'" Job cannot understand how the little sins of a little man can make any difference to God. Why doesn't He just pardon? It is almost Voltaire, who was echoed by others, "God will pardon me, that is His business."

Then Job tries to get the last laugh on God. He has to believe that he, though a man, matters to God, and like a little child he threatens with his disappearance. "You'll be sorry when I'm six feet under the ground," is another way to express verse 21: "For now I will lie down in the dust; and Thou wilt seek me, but I will not be.'" God will realize his error, but it will be too late, Job will be gone. Yet Job is really counting on the love of God—"thou wilt seek me"—even though nothing in Job's present condition seems to indicate that God cares.

Second Response to Eliphaz/Job 16 and 17

In the second cycle of speeches, Job is painfully aware of his abandonment by God and man. Eliphaz has resumed his charges, and Job can only respond, "Miserable comforters are you all." But he fiercely holds to his innocence of any kind of sin that could merit such scandalous treatment.

Job 16:1-17   Abandoned by God and Man   Job

maintains that if roles were reversed he would not treat a sufferer so—always an easy statement, but difficult to prove (vv. 4,5). Job pictures himself as a victim of attack by a wild animal (v. 9) and as a helpless object of the wrath of a fierce soldier (v. 14). Yet Job doggedly holds to his innocence (v. 17).

Job 16:18—17:9   Job's Witness in Heaven   This is one of the great bursts of light in the book. We shall identify three great figures which Job uses to identify his hope before God. In the chronology of the book this is actually the second figure. The first is in Job's answer to Bildad in 9:33. There Job longs for an "umpire." Here Job cries, "O earth, do not cover my blood'" (v. 18). He is saying that when his blood is poured out on the ground, he does not want it covered. His life-blood will continue to cry out, even after he is dead. (Cf. Gen 4:10 and Ezek. 24:7.) There is a "witness" for him in heaven. Some have thought the witness to be God the Father. Yet this does not seem to fit well in context. Job demands a representative to hear his case before God the Father. What an amazing foreshadowing of Jesus Christ!

Job 17:10-16   Job Anticipates Death   Job refuses all offers of hope for restoration. All is lost, Sheol is before him.

Third Response to Eliphaz/Job 23; 24:1-17,25

A textual problem is the reason for this unusual division of verses. Job 24:18-24 is virtually an impossible paragraph if the words are Job's. It is exactly what the friends have been saying about him all along. One version solves the problem by inserting the words "You say" at the beginning of verse 18 so that Job is supposedly giving the sentiments of his friends and not his own. Some have suggested they are the words of Zophar, who otherwise, for some unknown reason, does not appear in the third cycle of speeches.

Job 23:1-17   God Inaccessible   Job repeats his desire for a confrontation with God to present his case. God would hear and acquit him (vv. 6,7). But God is completely hidden from Job. What a contrast to Psalm 139. Job can find God nowhere! Yet he believes God knows his integrity and Job will "come forth as gold" (v. 10).

Job 24:1-17,25   God Inactive   Job sees life as evidence of injustice. The rich oppress the poor, whether rural or urban. It is interesting to note Job's analysis of injustice in the city. It has a very modern sound (vv. 12-17). Job's conclusion (v. 25) still shows the arrogance by which he keeps up his defenses. He knows that his professed innocence is inconsistent with his calamity.

Hardly a verse that we have included does not have textual problems and alternate readings. For those that seem unclear, other versions and more detailed commentaries will assist.

6
bilious Bildad

THE SPEECHES OF BILDAD/JOB 8; 18; 25

We now turn to Friend Number Two, Bildad the
Shuhite, and his three encounters with Job. He was
probably younger than Eliphaz, but he tries to seem
older by putting high value on old ideas. Although
his name means "Darling of God," this does not at
all make him more gracious, and Job suffers at his
hand. Like Eliphaz, Bildad champions orthodoxy,
and would probably have been willing to destroy
Job's body to save his soul.

Bildad's First Speech/Job 8

Bildad has just listened to the exchange between
Job and Eliphaz. Eliphaz had pressed the issue that
mortal men cannot be righteous before God (Job
4:17). Job had not only refused to accept the idea
but had implied that God was wrong in hounding
him so and watching his every move (Job 7:20). Between Eliphaz's accusations and Job's shocking im-

47

petuous words, the exchange was at best a draw. So Bildad comes out swinging.

Job 8:1-7   Affirmation of Divine Justice   As far as Bildad is concerned, Job is nothing more than a very large windbag (v. 2). The idea that God perverted His own justice was impossible for Bildad to take (v. 3).

Instead, he draws the heartless, cruel conclusion that Job's children must have sinned and that their punishment was therefore most appropriate. Remember that Job himself had presumed upon the possibility of secret sin on the part of his children and offered sacrifices for them (Job 1:5). Job can hardly accept the idea that all of his children had all sinned so heinously that all had been destroyed at once.

Bildad's alternative idea is even more incriminating. The sins of the fathers can be visited upon the children. In Israel there was the proverb which said, "The fathers have eaten sour grapes and the children's teeth are set on edge." Bildad doesn't spell out his accusation in so many words, but the suggestion is clear enough.

Both Jeremiah (Jer. 31:29,30) and Ezekiel (Ezek. 18:2-4) refuted this claim, pointing out that ultimately the responsibility for a man's sin rests on his own shoulders. But the concept of establishing moral responsibility in parent-child relationships still causes problems today. Naive acceptance by Christian parents of "Train up a child in the way he should go, and when he is old he will not depart from it"[2] (Prov. 22:6) as an unconditional promise rather than a general statement of principle has led to much agonized self-incrimination. This has been subtly reinforced by uncritical acceptance of a Freudian psychology that says neurotic problems in the adult are the result of repressions or unwise actions by the parent.

It is possible, of course, for irresponsible parents to cripple or maim the inner person of their children. Nevertheless, Job is pertinent in showing that family situations are not subject to easy analysis, either theologically or psychologically. Bildad puts the theological knife to a good father's heart and cruelly twists it.

Job 8:8-19   The Wisdom of the Past   Whereas Eliphaz had appealed to his own mystic revelations and the wisdom gleaned from his own class or group, Bildad resorts to the time-honored academic and religious strategy of appeal to ancient authority.

This is not to be scorned. The Christian and the Jew are constantly recalling and re-presenting the past. The perennial problem is how to properly conserve cherished values from the past and yet innovate boldly. Perhaps the key is in understanding that the true nature of biblical memory is always sacramental and creative, as demonstrated in the Passover meal, the Communion, or Easter. This is the difference between a mausoleum and a library or a community center. We must especially remember that the lessons of the past may be ambiguous, that the material must be carefully evaluated to keep it from shackling us. A quarry brings material from the past, but it is for building.

Although Bildad was adept in wisdom archaeology, he mouthed a tradition that erected an insurmountable barrier to the free flow of experimentation or new understanding. There are plenty of Bildads still present in the church; some even get put on boards.

Bildad's method—typical—is to quote a wise saying that presumably needs no proof. "Where there's smoke, there's fire," is the equivalent of verse 11, "Can the papyrus grow up without marsh?" Because Job's got trouble, right there in Uz, sin is somewhere on the premises.

Job 8:20-22 Summary of Hope Bildad, since it is his first speech, has not given up hope for Job. All will be well if Job will repent and take the good advice of such fine friends. "He will yet fill your mouth with laughter, and your lips with shouting'" (v. 21).

Bildad's Second Speech/Job 18

It is time for a response from Bildad but he really has nothing more to say. Yet he can hope that a repeated and even more florid picture of the wicked and his fate will bring Job to his senses. Bildad is a traditionalist, and when the conflict introduces new material he has no recourse but to try and pull the discussion back to his familiar territory.

Job 18:1-4 A Defense of the Comforters Bildad is amazed at Job's refusal to listen to his friends. How can he be so blind as to ignore the wisdom being given to him? For Job to be right demands cosmic rearrangement and that will not happen (v. 4).

Job 18:5-21 The Fate of the Wicked A familiar refrain is repeated with a gruesome determination, and with the particular twist that characterizes

Bildad. Job has lost his children (Job 8:4) and this means that his "lamp goes out" (vv. 5,6). There was no judgment greater than for a man to have no progeny, since this was about the only "immortality" that had been determined up to that time. Several Old Testament stories make very clear this great desire for descendants. (See 2 Sam. 21:17; 1 Kings 11:36; 15:4; 2 Kings 8:19; Psalm 132:17.)

Bildad's Third Speech/Job 25:1-6; 26:5-13

The text of Bildad's third speech is very brief as it is presented in our present version. Many have suggested that Job 26:5-13 also belongs to Bildad. Although this poetic eulogy of the greatness of God does not seem to fit well with Job's reply in 26:1-4, it is the kind of statement that would seem appropriate from either Job or Bildad. There was never really any disagreement between Job and the friends on that subject! Since these verses follow naturally out of Bildad's comments in chapter 25, we will consider it under this section rather than with Job's answer.

Job 25:1-6   God Is Great; Man Is Insignificant Bildad waxes eloquent over man's puniness. "How much less man, who is a maggot, and the son of man, who is a worm"[2] (v. 6). It is extremely odd that Bildad himself does not find this a threatening statement. He directs it to Job to promote humility and repentance. But why is it not equally applicable and shattering to Bildad? One of the great weaknesses in religious authority is that it often considers itself immune from the very truth it applies so vigorously to others.

We probably don't agree with Bildad anyhow ,and

51

we must remember that he is not a source of divine revelation. What do we mean when we say that man is a worm? The cries of modern psychological authorities against such an evaluation would be long and loud. "Self-worth" is one of the watchwords, and even the second table of the Law is an injunction to love our neighbors *as ourselves*. (See Matt. 19:19.) Regarding both the neighbor and ourselves as worms or maggots is probably not the intent of the commandment.

The scriptural concept of "original sin" further complicates the picture. This assumption that all human nature is defiled from its beginning results in the absolute impossibility of unaided human righteousness and a lowered expectation of unaided human decision and action. All this flies pretty much in the face of the optimism psychologists or anthropologists have about the true condition of human reason and good will.

How does the Christian keep in tension (1) the biblical truth of man in the image of God, loved by God and with a potential for redemption and divine fellowship, and (2) the biblical truth of man's depravity and native bent for disobedience and sin? This is not a simple assignment. The Christian's only option is to affirm the goodness of God's creation without denying the alienation of man brought about by the fall and human sin.

Job 26:5-13 Eulogy to God's Greatness This poem about the power of God in nature is one of the most beautiful expressions of the book. Remember that it is a poem, and that it is not the source of astronomic truth. I have heard attempts to find amazing scientific truth in verse 7, "He stretches out the north over empty space and hangs the earth on nothing.'" The idea was presented that there is a "hole" in the "north" (whatever that might be) around the north star, and that Job also had insight into the suspension of the earth in space.

But if Job intended this section to be a catalogue of scientific truth about modern astronomy, then we face a problem with Job's use of "Rahab," in verse 12. According to ancient mythology, Rahab was the mythological dragon of Chaos, supposedly subdued at Creation. Certainly, the dragon Rahab has no relationship with modern astronomy. In the same way, if we interpret verse 7 according to the principles that keep it in context, we will see it as part of a magnificent poetic description of God's power.

JOB'S RESPONSES TO BILDAD/
   JOB 9; 10; 19; 26; 27
First Response to Bildad/Job 9 and 10

Though the Joban poet does his best to make the speeches of the friends ring with the sincerity of their orthodoxy, the grandeur of poetic power is reserved for these various speeches of Job. He is the tragic hero around which this book turns and these passages are some of the greatest in all of literature. The major ideas in this speech are clear. Job does not seem to answer Bildad, who has spoken of God's justice, as much as he answers Eliphaz, who questioned the possibility of man's acceptance with God, but called for repentance and good works.

Job 9:1-13 The Arbitrariness of God Job lifts a hymn of praise to the power of God (vv. 5-10) within a kind of skeptical parenthesis (vv. 1-4, 11-13) that shows his sarcastic response to this power. No one can stand against God, and Job certainly can't even find Him, no matter how powerful He is. By this very clever argument Job shifts the whole question that Eliphaz has raised. He said that God is sovereign and man is sinful. Job says that God is arbitrary and man is weak. It is not a question of ethical value but relative strength, and Job resents it.

Job 9:14-24 The Elusiveness of God Job in his despair attains to a pinnacle of effrontery and rebellion. Job will not submit to force, so he suggests that God is cowardly not to meet him on proper terms. God is pictured as an unscrupulous lawyer, catching Job in his own words. "I would have to implore the mercy of my Judge"[1] (v. 15). Finally Job throws up his hands. He is perfect, but it makes no difference. "He destroys the guiltless and the wicked. If the scourge kills suddenly, He mocks the despair of the innocent"[1] (vv. 22,23). We all shudder a bit at Job's statements, even though we are sympathetic with his grief. He flatly charges God with flagrant disregard of justice and responsibility. Job has made a very bad leap from life, as he sees it, to God as he presumes Him to be.

This is really blasphemous, but we must have patience with Job. He is probably at his lowest point. Thank God that this is not his final word and that none of us is judged until all the results are in! At least Job is thinking and wrestling with the issues. The friends don't blaspheme, but neither do they risk to open their eyes wide. They end up proper but wrong.

Job 9:25—10:7   The Inhumanness of God.   Job knows he will be found guilty. This is an interesting parody of Psalm 51:7, "Wash me, and I shall be whiter than snow." Job denies it, "if I should wash myself with snow and cleanse my hands with lye, yet Thou wouldst plunge me into the pit, and my own clothes would abhor me"' (vv. 30,31). God is the enemy, pushing us ruthlessly into the ditch, and all our cleaning up by our goodness or ceremonial purification is useless. God is not a man, and that makes their reconciliation virtually impossible (v. 32).

There follows in verse 33 one of the great flashes of insight of the Old Testament. "There is no umpire between us, who may lay his hand upon us both."' Job does not discover the answer, but he is brave enough to imagine the possibility and regret its lack. An "umpire" is not just a judge to bring God and man to trial. He is not just an arbiter or referee who would make a decision. Rather, he is one who can reconcile, who can place a hand upon both God and man. He is a mediator, an intermediary, and by implication he is one who would so relate to God and man, so be God and man that he could participate in the reality of both.

Job is not predicting the coming of Jesus, but it cannot be denied that in his misery he envisions the benefits of the Incarnation, the reconciling work of one who would be "very God of very God" and "very man of very man."

Without the mediator, Job knows that God is not responding to him, and he mocks God with the possibility that God is now imitating the wicked by condemning the innocent (Job 10:1-7).

Job 10:8-22   The Creativeness of God   Finally, Job contemplates the mystery of his own creation. He knows that God has formed him, and he would assume that God cannot hate what he makes. Yet since Job's life is filled with such relentless attack from God, against which he has no defenses, he sobs in his solitude and wonders why God ever allowed him to come from the womb.

Second Response to Bildad/Job 19

Job's answers to Bildad are unusually significant. We have considered Job's desire for a Mediator. In this section we have the most famous passage of the book—Job's affirmation of faith in his Redeemer. This completes the three great figures that speak so eloquently of Jesus—the Mediator (Job 9), the Witness (Job 16) and the Redeemer (Job 19).

Job 19:1-6   Job's Impatience with his Friends Bildad has just observed that people of the East and the West will be shocked at Job's condition (18:20) and Job can do no more than attempt to shame him with his oppressive words (v. 3).

Job 19:7-12   God's Assault on Job   Once more Job recounts the way God has stopped his every attempt at wholeness and integrity. He dramatically shouts, "Violence!" but like a person being attacked in a lonely place, no one comes to his aid (v. 7).

Job 19:13-22   Rejection by All   In a very poignant and moving passage, Job catalogs the various persons who now scorn him. No one has rallied to his help. Relatives, friends, trusted servants, his wife, his brothers, even the youngsters now mock him. Especially cutting is the sorry treatment from these friends. "Pity me, pity me, O you my friends, for the hand of God has struck me!" (v. 21).

There is always a certain sense of solitude in suffering. Many times the sufferer has to be isolated just for the well-being of the healthier part of society. But the natural development of the suffering itself can also bring solitude.

When the problem is all-consuming, the sufferer's psychic energies are totally dedicated to the self. This is a most difficult circumstance and often tends to become habitual when we suffer a long time. Perhaps that is why we need praying, concerned friends who will help us keep perspective and be sensitive to the needs of others.

Job 19:23-29 Assurance of Vindication We have said that this is probably the best known passage of the book. "I know that my Redeemer liveth" has been memorialized by Handel, if in no other fashion. This passage, as we shall see, is looked to as one of the greatest pivotal words on the theme of resurrection.

Every commentator will immediately note that the text of this passage is extremely difficult, leaving open possibilities for several different readings. Almost any Bible of recent publication will have an array of footnotes and marginal readings.

The textual problems notwithstanding, this is a passage of amazing hope and beauty. At the very least Job feels that his case with God will be resolved to his satisfaction and that he will be granted a vision of God. At the very most Job has a deep presentiment that he will in some marvelous way live with God in a new physical reality—a lightning flash, however vague and fleeting, that illumines the great truth of the resurrection of the body. This is the same truth seen in its full glory in the reality of Christ's resurrection.

In examining the text we will follow the *New American Standard Bible* translation and indicate where the differences in translation could occur.

"Oh, that my words were written! Oh, that they were inscribed in a book! That with an iron stylus and lead they were engraved in the rock forever!" Job senses the importance of what he is going to say. He deeply desires that it be written down for posterity and preserved. Then comes his resounding affirmation, "As for me, I know that my Redeemer lives."

There is some question as to exactly what he means. Who is the "Redeemer"? Is it the God with whom he is arguing so frankly? Or is it the Witness, the Mediator, whom he longs for to take his case before God?

The Hebrew word *go'el,* which is here translated "Redeemer" has many meanings in the Old Testament. Most frequently, it refers to the next of kin who was required to continue the family of a dead man or have first option on his estate. (See Deut. 25:5-10; Ruth 2:20; 3:9; 4:4.) Sometimes it refers to the one who sought to avenge the blood of a killed relative. (See 2 Sam. 14:11; Josh. 20:3-6.) The word is also a title for God, describing his relationship to Israel. (See Exod. 6:6; Isaiah 41:14.) Only once is there a specific reference to God as a personal "Redeemer," in the sense of "my Redeemer" (Psalm 19:14), although in other references the verb form is used to picture God as doing the redeeming (Psalm 69:18). This combination of ideas describes a defender of the oppressed. So Job is saying, "I know that Someone lives who will defend me in my oppression."

But we still have the question: Is the Redeemer God? Is Job saying, "I know my God lives?" or is he saying, "I know someone lives who will avenge me, who will vindicate me?"

Scholars are divided on this. Some feel that the Redeemer is not actually God the Father in Job's mind. That is, Job is not saying, "I know that God lives." Rather, they feel that Job is again referring to the Witness, the Mediator, whom he mentioned earlier. Verse 26 seems to back this up, where Job seems to suggest that the Redeemer is the agent by which he shall see God.

However, Job is also longing for vindication. He feels that he is being unjustly accused and persecuted. He believes that he must ultimately be vindicated. If no man can vindicate him, then the only one who can must be God. So he is saying, "I know that the One who will vindicate me lives."

If we combine the two ideas, we see Job saying: "I know that only God can vindicate me, and I know that someone must plead my case before God." From our point of view, we see his longing fulfilled in the person of Christ, who was both God and man, who alone can vindicate, but who also pleads our case before the Father on the basis of His shed blood. Job does not have to understand all this. It awaited the light of Christ.

Another textual problem brings us to the issue of

when Job expects this vindication to take place. In verse 25, the Hebrew reads, "he will stand upon the dust." This could mean the dust of Job's dead body. Verse 26 is extremely difficult. There is equal textual reason to read, "Without my flesh I shall see God," as well as, "From my flesh I shall see God." So Job could be saying that he expects to be vindicated at the moment of his death when he expects to see God. These verses also suggest that he will be alive to see God and be vindicated *after* his death. Job is so astounded in thinking of this prospect that he exclaims, "My heart faints within me!" (v. 27).

This is an important breakthrough, especially since there is so little clear statement in the Old Testament of eternal life or even life after death at all. Job desires to see God and he believes that when he does it will be him seeing God and not some disembodied spirit who isn't the real Job. In other words, he is looking forward to conscious physical, personal life after death.

What an amazing progression in Job's thought! Not only does the need for Christ emerge, and not only does Job reach out for a life beyond death, but he also reaches to God and a vision of Him as the ultimate solution of all his confusion and misery. Although God eventually speaks to Job, rather than appearing to him, Job will be able to say when it is all over, "Now my eye sees Thee" (Job 42:5).

Third Response to Bildad/Job 26:1-4; 27:1-6

Note the textual problem surrounding the arrangement of material in chapters 26 and 27. We are assuming that part of chapter 26 (vv. 5-14) is the conclusion of the speech of Bildad, and that part of chapter 27 (vv. 7-23) is the third speech of Zophar.

Job 26:1-4 Job's Scorn for Bildad This is a burst of sarcasm. Job wants Bildad to know what a miserable failure he has been both in bringing a convincing case and in providing comfort for a sufferer.

Job 27:1-6 Job's Relentless Protest of Innocence What a disappointment to these tireless debaters to discover that their objective has been so totally unattained. Job is no closer to repentance or capitulation than when they started, and from the sound of this paragraph, he will never change.

7

zealous Zophar

THE SPEECHES OF ZOPHAR/JOB 11; 20; 27

Zophar the Naamathite is the third friend of Job in this little company of commiseration. It's difficult to be the third man in each cycle, but our poet gives him some most interesting dialogue and gives Job some most helpful responses.

Zophar is probably the coarsest and most cruelly outspoken of the "comforters." This may be in part due to his appearance in the third spot. He has more fuel for the fire of frustration and he is almost forced to extremes in order to gain any attention at all. In one sense he has nothing new to contribute theologically, so his only avenue of innovation is emotional. The contrast is interesting.

Eliphaz has approached Job as the well-ordered, polite man of composure and experience. He is empirical, in that he claims that his ideas have been tested in the arena of action. He is a pseudo-mystic, with

63

his supernatural revelations, and he speaks as an institutional, establishment man. Bildad is the authoritarian who claims the sanction of time-honored wisdom, the friend of the ancients, with a proverb for every problem. Zophar does not just speak, he pounces. He attacks. He presents, as we shall see, the kind of argument that allows for no dissension or debate.

Zophar's First Speech/Job 11

Each of the friends reasons from a theological posture, and this first speech of Zophar establishes him as the man most aware of the transcendence of God.

Job 11:1-6 Job's Iniquity Zophar has listened to Job refuse the statements of Eliphaz and Bildad. He can barely restrain himself, and sweeps aside everything that Job has said. "A multitude of words," "babble,"² is his description for Job's argument (vv. 2,3). He finds Job's protest of innocence infuriating. He plunges to a new depth of invective in his first paragraph by saying that God is not punishing Job to the degree that his sin and disobedience really deserve (v. 6)!

Zophar sees the answer to Job's problem in the secret wisdom of God. If God would only speak to Job and open to him these secret sources of understanding (vv. 5,6)! Zophar implies that he has access to these secret fountains of wisdom, and that he knows all the hidden things which should be known. However Zophar chooses not to reveal his secrets to Job. It is enough for Job to be aware that Zophar knows!

How often this kind of attitude is found in Christian leaders and teachers. How many talk about the "deep" things of God, often in a "deep" and rather mystical voice, and make one feel that these are spiritual secrets which some have and others don't. It is usually they who do and you who don't!

The New Testament, though not a simple book, is certainly not a secret one either. The wisdom of God for meaningful life is not in some mysterious, unrecognizable formula, but plainly given for childlike acceptance and obedience.

Job 11:7-12 God's Infinity This passage gives a brilliant statement of the power and majesty of God. God's transcendence reaches completely beyond our human dimensions and limitations. There is nothing wrong with the ideas, but it seems strange that Zophar does not find God's great transcendence threatening to his own pride and inadequacy. Strangely enough, he assumes that he is perfectly all right, and that somehow he has become acceptable to this infinite God.

Zophar concludes this section with an interesting proverb that is rather difficult in its text and application (v. 12). "A stupid man will get understanding, when a wild ass's colt is born a man"[2]—which will never happen. As far as Zophar is concerned, Job is obviously the stupid man.

Job 11:13-20 Reward for Repentance Now the real coin of his realm becomes apparent. He has talked about the infinite God, but he has nothing to suggest for Job but repentance and reform. "If you would direct your heart right,"[1] (v. 13) is just like saying to Job, "Get right with God, and all this trouble will be over." Prayer and right living—piety and morality—these are the fees for salvation. "Your life would be brighter than noonday"' (v. 17).

There are two equivalents of this in our modern religious life. One is the works-righteousness man who says that people really get what is coming to them and what God wants from any one is a good life, hurting as few as possible, helping as many as you can. The other is the "simple gospel" man, to whom doubt is sin, a neurosis is backsliding, and his simple answer to the most complex questions is usually, "Pray and get involved in church work," or "Let God take over your life."

This is not to say that the second man is not of some help to the church. He has a way of challenging our superficial complications, our easy resort to the abstract, our over-intellectualizing of problems which may be rather fundamental. Yet he is so often a hindrance to the searching and tortured soul, and his cliches and pat answers can drive more sensitive persons right up the wall!

Zophar's Second Speech/Job 20

Job 20:1-19 The Short Triumph and Certain Doom of the Wicked Theme and variations: the awful fate of the wicked is coupled with the variations of coarseness as Zophar elaborates on how quickly that doom will come.

We must remember that Job has just finished the magnificent statement of 19:23-29, "I know that my Redeemer lives." Yet the startling impact of this sublime passage is lost on Zophar, probably because of the jarring ending: "If you say, 'How we will pursue

him!' and, 'The root of the matter is found in him';
be afraid of the sword, for wrath brings the punishment of the sword, that you may know there is a
judgment"[2] (Job 19:28,29). Job has thrown down
the gauntlet and frankly advised these friends that
they had better worry about the judgment of God on
themselves!

No wonder Zophar splutters "I listened to the reproof which insults me"[1] (Job 20:3). He did catch
on. There are various possible divisions for this
chapter of doom, but it is really all on one piece—
"the triumphing of the wicked is short" (v. 5). The
crudeness appears in the way Zophar described that
quickness. "Though his height mount up to the heavens, and his head reach to the clouds, he will perish
forever like his own dung"[2] (vv. 6,7).

In verses 12-15 Zophar likens wickedness to
something sweet in the mouth but immediately turning sour in the stomach, only to be vomited out
again. All this seems to have little to do with Job,
whose experience, though difficult, is hardly parallel.

About the only thing Zophar can muster is a wild
accusation that would be easy enough against a rich
man: he has ruthlessly seized property for his gain
(v. 19). The remainder of the chapter is a dismal rehearsal of doom, with an almost grisly description of
God piercing the wicked with a bronze arrow. "It is
drawn forth and comes out his back, even the glittering point from his gall"[1] (v. 25).

Zophar doesn't need any facts. God judges the
wicked man quickly, and that's that! Job has been
shouting back with a red face that God doesn't work
that way, but Zophar is unaffected. Job will bitterly

react to this simplistic analysis of human experience.

Zophar's Third Speech

Job 27:7-23   The State and the Fate of the God-less.   This passage does not seem appropriate for Job unless he is ironically giving what he knows to be the views of his advisors. It is similar to Job 24:18-24, which we referred to in the "Second Response to Eliphaz". In this instance the sentiment is not Job's, and can be considered with the material of Zophar.

The judgment of God upon the wicked is total. His children are slaughtered or starving, his riches are vanished, his house is swept away like a spider's web, terrors overtake him, and a whirlwind carries him off in the middle of the night (vv. 14-20).

JOB'S RESPONSES TO ZOPHAR/ JOB 12; 13; 14; 21

When Zophar finishes his first speech and all three friends have spouted their party line of retributive justice, Job knows that the gulf between him and them is fixed. But Job will reply anyhow, shouting his defiance and longing for vindication. This speech is the longest response Job makes to any one statement. It contains another amazing conclusion.

First Response to Zophar/Job 12—14

Job 12:1-25   Recognition of God's Power and Wisdom   Job must first handle these miserable comforters (vv. 1-6). His opening remark sets the tone. "No doubt you are the people, and wisdom will die with you"[2] (v. 2). Job is bitter in his remembrance that his many prayers have brought him to the ash-heap, even though he has been just and blameless. He mocks his friends who from their safe vantage points look so easily and contemptuously upon his misfortune (v. 5). Pinpointing the inconsistency of their argument about retributive justice, Job contends that those who practice evil live in peace, even those who commit idolatry (v. 6).

Then Job acknowledges that all the affairs of men are brought about by the power of God. None withstands him, and nations rise and fall only at his command. Job is showing these friends that he knows the right words, can put together the right phrases. He can be as orthodox as anyone (vv. 12-25). Yet there is a certain sarcasm in all this, and Job is going to be courageous enough to contend with God over the whole business.

Job 13:1-16   Job's Rebuke to His Friends   Zophar had classified Job as a "stupid man" (Job 11:12). Considering Job's place in his family and community, this was probably the unkindest cut of all. A "wise" man, as Job was supposed to be, just cannot stand this kind of attack. So he turns on Zophar and puts him in his place. "What you know, I also know; I am not inferior to you. As for you, you whitewash with lies; worthless physicians are you all"[2] (Job 13:2,4). "Zophar," says Job, "your ridiculous proverbs and cheap defenses are as worthless as ashes and clay" (v. 12). Job is getting up courage to challenge God. He knows in advance that challenging God is not only risky, but probably hopeless.

It is in this setting that we encounter Job 13:15, so nobly but inaccurately translated in the *King James Version* as, "Though he slay me, yet will I trust in him." The problem is a poor translation of the Hebrew for "hope" translated as "trust" and a wrong translation of the Hebrew word *lo* which with one marking means "him", but with another means "not" or "no". The word *yet* in the *King James* phrase, "Yet will I trust in him," does not appear in the Hebrew at all.

A more accurate reading, found in the *American Standard Version* and substantiated in the leading commentaries, reads, "Behold, he will slay me: I have no hope: Nevertheless, I will maintain my ways before him." With the traditional translation, the statement of arrogance in the second phrase of the verse would be completely incomprehensible following the statement of unconditional hope in the first phrase.

Certainly this text, as translated in the *King James Version* has helped many people in times of great distress. Nevertheless, we must accept the more accurate translation. Respect for the Scripture always brings delight, rather than disappointment, in discovering its true meaning.

In verse 16, Job says the only thing that can save him in his direct challenge to God is his genuine godliness.

Job 13:18—14:22 Job's Challenge to God
Now begins one of the sublime poems of the book. Job moves away from these disappointing friends and dares to challenge God. He knows that he takes his life in his hand, but he is so confident of his cause that he offers to die quietly if anyone with integrity can contend against him (v. 19).

In verses 20 and 21 Job asks God to restrain Himself and to allow him the freedom to speak openly, either as plaintiff or as defendant. Now, like some Elijah calling for an answer from God, he hurls his challenge: "How many are my iniquities and my sins? Make me know my transgression and my sin"² (v. 23). One can imagine a great dramatic pause in Job's speech. He waits for a reply, for a thunderbolt, for some response—there is nothing. "Why dost Thou hide Thy face?"³ (v. 24).

Job then moves into his complaint against man's sorry history. Man is "of few days, and full of trouble"⁴ (Job 14:1). What is the point of bringing such a temporal creature into judgment? Since the race is defiled, what is the point of looking for anything from any man (vv. 3,4)? This is an unworthy procedure for God to take. Better for God just to look away, and give man his brief day unmolested.

The big problem for Job is death. A cut-down tree has hope but not a man. He is gone, like a dried-up lake (vv. 7-12). Then Job has a startling suggestion. Could it be that God would somehow preserve Job in Sheol and then at a set time, call him back? "If a man dies, will he live again"⁵ (v. 14)? Job fantasizes on what that recall would be—no more surveillance of sins, transgressions and iniquities sealed up and covered over (vv. 15-17).

What Job talks about is not a resurrection as such; it is not eternal life; it is certainly not immortality of the soul; nor is it an assertion of a right to immortality or a need for justice beyond the grave. It is a momentary longing and crying for existence. This is a progression from the desire for nothingness in Job 3.

Think of the meaning in this statement, "Thou wilt

call, and I will answer Thee; Thou wilt long for the work of Thy hands'" (v. 15). This is the awareness of a need to commune with God, a call for love.

The Hebrew had concentrated on the blessedness of the present and the continuation of life through the family and the covenant people. Since Job now has nothing in either of these areas, he reaches out honestly for a loving God beyond death. The Hebrew had a kind of optimism about life, that it was good, especially if man was obedient and God blessed him. Death was obvious, but unreal, and largely minimized. This was not enough for Job.

The parallel today is striking. With humanistic optimism life is seen as worthwhile, but there is an almost paranoid evasion of and a tacit denial of death. The hope that Job dared have for a moment is the constant possession of the Christian and the good news of life in Christ to a world that still has a one hundred percent mortality rate!

Yet Job's daring hope of awakening is lost on the ash-heap of reality. Just as water wears away the stones, so God allows the hope of man to be destroyed (v. 19). What can there be for Job but more pain and finally death? He has challenged God and dreamed of release, but all for naught.

Second Response to Zophar/Job 21

The reply to Zophar's second speech brings clearly into the open Job's challenge to moral order in the world. The assumption that only the wicked suffer is nailing him to the wall. So he leaves his own case and his desire for God's vindication to take a hard look at the world around him.

72

Job 21:1-6   A Brief Introduction   Job silences his friends, hoping that this silence will be some consolation, after which they will be free to mock on (v. 3). Job's complaint is not really against them or any other man. It is far larger than that.

Job 21:7-34   The Prosperity of the Wicked Verse 7 is a kind of text for this little sermon: "Why do the wicked still live, continue on, also become very powerful?" The rest of the chapter elaborates. The wicked have houses, flocks, and an abundance of children. They finally experience a peaceful death (vv. 8-13). In the midst of all this they freely scoff at religion. It is not a case of wondering whether they "serve God for naught"; they don't serve him at all, but the blessings keep rolling in! They decided long ago that prayer is pointless (vv. 14-16).

Job quickly puts down the anticipated theological bromide that God will punish them through the calamities of their children. It's meaningless, says Job. What possible difference can it make to a dead man if all the trouble he deserves comes after he has lived a rich and easy—and wicked—life. *Apres moi, le deluge* (After me, the flood) is hard to fight (vv. 17-21).

When Job looks around there is no evidence of even-handed justice in the world. The wicked man dies prosperous; another man, wicked or righteous, dies in misery with nothing good to look back on. The worms get them both (vv. 22-26).

So there can be no conclusion but that the wicked man is spared from calamity and goes in pomp and circumstance to a peaceful sleep. "The clods of the valley are sweet to him" (v. 33), is the fulfillment of a very common folk saying, *Sic tibi terra levis* (May the earth lie on you lightly). If the friends don't believe this, they should just talk to some people who have been around (vv. 27-34).

The force of Job's argument in context must have been great, even though no one acknowledged it. Job is poking at something that always needs attention—the tendency of religious people to tailor or ignore the facts of human experience in order to fit them into the framework of their own theological ideas.

When Galileo looked through his telescope and saw that the moon was a rough and irregular body, he said so, and invited the princes of the church to take a look. They had already taught that "heavenly" bodies were perfect crystalline spheres, and they had scriptures to prove it. Their reaction was to pronounce Galileo a heretic and to refuse to look in that horrible telescope.

In many other ways, especially with the advancing knowledge of modern times, the Christian has unnecessarily gone on the defensive. We must love the truth, not just our definitions of it. The Bible is never well-served by blind and rabid defense. Neither is it necessary to quickly yield to every new philosophic or scientific fad or theory! It is possible to toss pearls to swine! Yet Christians must be open and honest people, willing to look at truth wherever it might arise, willing to admit ignorance when the answer just isn't available.

What should be said about Job's argument? Do the wicked prosper and the righteous suffer? Human experience says yes, and the Bible says yes. God's blessings come "on the just and on the unjust"

(Matt. 5:45). The Christian is to expect suffering (see 2 Tim. 3:12). The church lifts its voice in worship, "The glorious company of the martyrs praise thee." It is obvious that the righteous may end up quite violently.

This does not, however, prove what Job seemed to be implying—that there is no moral order in the universe. Two things must be remembered: First, Scripture teaches that the righteous judgment of God comes to man beyond this life. Job did not know this, though he reached out for it. Second, to the extent that the will of God is taken seriously in the society of man, the righteous are blessed and the wicked suffer.

Since this is an evil world, not committed to the obedience of God, wrong can seem to be forever on the throne and truth can seem to be forever on the scaffold. But the promise to the Christian is that God will work together with him in all things for good (see Rom. 8:28). Everything is not good, but God will work with us in everything.

So both Job and his comforters were wrong. Had Job been well and prosperous, he probably would have taken the same stance as his friends. But now he was in a better position than they were to discover the truth and find consolation and meaning, because he had been plunged head-on into the sticky circumstances of experience. And it was only from the perspective of experience that he became prone to criticizing and questioning the condition of moral order in the universe.

If we only look at experience, we will have plenty of reason to ask questions about moral order in the universe. Many things happen that are hard to explain. It is hard to explain why Manasseh, the wickedest king of Israel, ruled the longest. It is hard to explain why Hitler could die at his own hand in a flaming bunker in Berlin and Stalin could die of old age in his bed. Each of us, even on a personal level, has faced situations and seemingly meaningless experiences which have been hard, if not impossible, to explain.

In trying to find an explanation for inequities in the world of experience, Job denied that there is moral order in the universe. But it is not so much a matter of having to deny moral order in the universe as it is a willingness to let God be the governor of that order. Job needs new light here and—perhaps —new humility.

8
hymn to wisdom

When we come to chapter 28 the narrative shifts suddenly. In chapter 27, either we conclude with the words of Job in verse 6, "I hold fast my righteousness and will not let it go,"[1] or we have the final statement of the chapter, possibly from Zophar, "It claps its hands at him, and hisses at him from its place."[2] Neither of these alternatives seems to have any connection with the abrupt statement in 28:1, "Surely there is a mine for silver."[1]

It is difficult for us to speculate what the purpose of this hymn is, especially since the author does not make that purpose clear. The first verse of the next chapter shows that the speaker here is probably not Job. Then who is it? One reasonable alternative is the Joban poet, the author of this book, who for reasons which he did not disclose, felt that his total purpose would be best served by this insertion. The similarity of expressions between this chapter and chapters 38—42, the Voice from the Whirlwind, would give credence to this view.

The only other suggestion, which I reject for lack of any convincing evidence, is that this is a hymn by the poet, written at another time and put in here just so it would be preserved.

There are several good reasons for its appearance here. One of them is the long and involved debate that began with chapter three. The author may be sensitive to a reader's need and ability. He refreshes the mind by a purposeful diversion and then returns to the sequence again.

Another good reason is to comment indirectly on the argument of the friends, and anticipate the Voice from the Whirlwind. Since man (Job and his friends) is incapable of discovering wisdom, God alone must be revealed as the Source of wisdom. This makes the whirlwind a necessity.

The only weakness of this statement is that we are still to have a recapitulation by Job and a lengthy discussion from Elihu that sounds as though man has not given up the search for wisdom. But the author does not have to deal with Job and Elihu as though they have heard this hymn. Remember that this work is not a stenographic report of a conference. It is a creative piece of epic poetry constructed around a cast of participants speaking the understanding of the author who is an instrument of divine revelation.

A comparison has been made between this hymn and the chorus of a Greek play. Like a chorus this hymn provides comment or observation to give the audience deeper insight into the real issues of the drama, while the action on stage is suspended.

The hymn also exalts wisdom, reminding us of the nature of this book as wisdom literature. Proverbs, Ecclesiastes and a number of the Psalms are in this same category. Wisdom literature usually takes the form of pithy sayings and practical maxims. The whole point of the material is to produce a practical piety, a guide for daily living.

Wisdom in Job, however, is more profound and mysterious, reminding us of Proverbs 8:22-31, where Wisdom is personified as the joyous associate with God in creation. The whole approach in Job is far more philosophic. In fact, Job's encounters with the maxims and pithy sayings, especially from Bildad, are nothing short of exasperating.

With these introductory observations we can look at the hymn in detail. There are three stanzas.

Job 28:1-13 Man's Technological Skill The poet begins his discourse by describing man's uncanny ability to ferret out valuable metals from the almost inaccessible depths of the earth. He dramatically describes the activity of mining. The miners penetrate the darkness, far from man's normal habitat. They suspend themselves in precarious spots, far below the unsuspecting field where grain is sprouting (vv. 3-6), and where birds and beasts never come vv. 7-8). The miner even diverts streams to find the precious metals (vv. 9-11).

The poet has selected an impressive conquest of nature for his *gloria in excelsis homini*. Mining was an amazing feat for man in those bygone days, equivalent to some of our technological advances today. The warning of the poet was that man should not be fooled by his marvelous accomplishments.

It seems that man's technical skills have always far out-stripped his personal skills. It is humbling to be reminded that we can fly to the moon and back, but often not walk a street at night in safety. A discerning British doctor pointed out to me that the world's leading pediatrics and obstetrics hospital is located at the heart of an American metropolitan area that has one of the highest infant mortality rates in the Western world. Our technology is not necessarily the key to well-being. We do not know as yet whether our nuclear science will save us or destroy us. We are horrified to discover that our supposed advances create massive new problems which we are not prepared to deal with.

The Joban poet is impressed with technological man, but he tells us that technology is not the road to wisdom and understanding. Far from being man "come of age," our present society seems barely adolescent.

Job 28:14-22 The Futile Search for Wisdom Since wisdom cannot be bought nor discovered, the search now turns to mystic and cultic sources. The deep (abyss) and the sea are personified (v. 14) as is Sheol (v. 22). The abyss is the great reservoir of water underground that acts as resource for the seas. It is linked with chaos of Genesis 1. "Abaddon" (Job 28:22; 26:6) another name for Sheol, is found frequently in wisdom literature. In none of these places can wisdom be found.

The reference that all kinds of gold and jewels will not purchase wisdom seems to relate to the elaborate burial rites of Egypt and Mesopotamia. Nowhere is wisdom to be found and no creature has discovered it.

80

Job 28:23-28 Wisdom Known Only to God
There is only one answer remaining. This wisdom
is known to God only. He established and ordained
it at the time of creation. (This is a parallel to
Prov. 8:22-31 , mentioned earlier.)

The question now becomes whether or not God
has revealed this place of wisdom to man. Verse 28
says yes: "The fear of the Lord, that is wisdom; and
to depart from evil is understanding."

There are many who just cannot feel that this
verse was really the work of the Joban poet. They
point out that this is the only place in the book where
the Hebrew word *adonai* is used for God. To some
the verse seems to retreat from the tone of Job back
to a limited ethical regulation, which is conventional
and prosaic, similar to references in Proverbs (3:5;
14:16; 16:16) and Ecclesiastes (12:13).

But that argument overlooks the grandeur of this
statement, even though it is couched in simple and
familiar terms. The writer of Ecclesiastes explores all
human attainment and knowledge and decides that
the whole matter is to fear God and keep his com-
mandments. The same pattern is given in Job 1:1, so
certainly the writer of Job was aware of it. Therefore, it hardly seems likely that this verse was inter-
polated by some later writer. To dismiss it arbitrarily
without more convincing evidence seems unnecessary.

Then why is the verse there? Could it mean that
man, with all his resourcefulness, may search for wisdom but never find true meaning and reality until he
accepts the simple fact that life is found in fearing
God and turning away from evil? Could it be that the
poet is steering us back to the truth, away from the

peripheral arguments put forth by both Job and his friends? Since this fear of God in its highest sense has not been evident in any of their lives, perhaps the author wants to reassure us that the answer is coming. He could be leading up to the Whirlwind, which will give a new dimension of meaning to the command to fear God.

9
summation for the defense

Just as Job began the debate with a soliloquy, so now he closes the debate with a soliloquy. Just as the first one was addressed to God, rather than to his friends, so was the last.

We will not hear from the friends again. For some time they have had nothing more to say. This closing speech shows how dismally they failed in their efforts to break this stubborn rebel.

In this lengthy speech, the past is somewhat glamorized by remembrance and virtue is enhanced by distance. But Job's recital of his own virtue is not relieved by even the slightest hint of humility or inadequacy. Our sympathies are with Job because of his terrible suffering and tragic losses; nevertheless, in this speech he comes across as naive or nauseating or perhaps a bit of both.

Job easily moves into the past and recalls the beautiful time when all was well.

Job 29:1-10 Former Happiness He remembers the former blessing of God. In the months of old, when Job was at the zenith of his power, God was with him. The term "autumn days" in verse 4 does not mean for Job what it usually means for us. For him "autumn" was the time of ripeness of days. It was a mellow, fruitful, happy season when righteous man could reap the proper benefits of what he had sown.

The memory of his children is still far too keen to allow him more than a line, "And my children were around me"' (v. 5). Job was respected by young and old. When he took his place at the city gate with the rulers, everyone waited to hear his opinion (vv. 9,10).

Job 29:11-17 Former Benevolence Job also remembers the many ways he had shared his blessing with those in need. Here, and again in Job 31, he makes it clear that he took very seriously the ethical implications of his obedience to God as it affected the poor and distressed. Job befriended the poor, the fatherless, the sick, the widow, the blind, the lame, even the oppressed who was not an acquaintance or responsibility (vv. 12-16). Job knew that righteousness was not a cultic conformity alone, but love and mercy to those cast out and uncared for.

The lesson is unavoidable. The age of the gospel has not altered this principle. God still cares for those who are oppressed or deprived. Whether the weak and powerless of the world be orphans and widows of Job's day, or those who were born in the wrong race, lack education, suffer from malnutrition or incapacity in our day, they are still the concern of the Christian.

Job 29:18-20 Former Expectations Given the theology that formed him, what could Job expect but to "die in the nest," with his children about him after living a long and full life? He was a man of virility and power at the time of his trial. We tend to think that Job was an old man. This is not so. His sons and daughters are not pictured as married. The statement in verse 8 that even the aged elders stood up in Job's presence would be pointless if he had been as old as they. In Job 15:10 Eliphaz and his friends claim to be older than Job's father. The trial was even more difficult physically because Job was cut down at the time of his physical and personal prowess. Now all this is but a memory.

Job 29:21-23 Former Esteem These verses complement verses 7-10. Job is not unaware of the significant place he occupied among his peers. Job knew it, and loved it. Everyone waited for Job's opinion. Job's optimistic spirit was an encouragement to all, and he was like a king among the troops. The ending to verse 25 is difficult textually but seems understandably cutting: "as one who comforted the mourners." The three friends might cringe at that statement.

PRESENT SUFFERING/JOB 30

"But now," is the sad reality of Job's present condition. He is rudely brought back from his reverie to the boils and the ash heap. Repetition of the phrase at verse 9 and verse 16, indicates three stanzas commenting on different aspects of his misery. He concludes with a lament on the inequity of his treatment in view of his own responses to people in need.

Job 30:1-8   The Base Men Who Now Despise Job   The description of those who now make sport of Job is a caustic one. These are the rabble, not just the poor. Some of what Job says about these people can be credited to his bitterness from suffering, and we will excuse his sounds of bigotry. Yet it is not a truism that to be poor is to be virtuous. Job was not without powers of discernment to see the treachery and stupidity of some people.

The vicious reactions of peasant populations the world around is legendary, especially if there is reason to believe someone is cursed by God. When Job was thrown on the ash heap, the refuse pile, outside the city, undoubtedly some poor illiterates were overjoyed, and they now taunted this once-powerful leader.

Job's sorrow was to be outcast by the outcasts. This has often been the experience of good men. Paul comments that he and the apostles became "as the scum of the world, the dregs of all things"[1] (1 Cor. 4:13). In view of Job's sincere aid for the poor in time of his power and wealth (Job 29:11-17), this cruel response was especially difficult for him to bear.

Job 30:9-15   Present Indignities   Job seems to find no human source of comfort, nor divine source either, for that matter. He describes his shambles in a picturesque phrase, "God has loosed my cord and humbled me"[2] (v. 11). The cord may be either the bow string to signify Job's loss of power or it may be a tent cord, indicating the disarray into which his life has now fallen.

Job 30:16-23   Present Despondency   Here is a vivid and moving description of Job's physical suffering—days of affliction, nights racked with incessantly gnawing pain. Job is hopeless, for it is God who has cast him into the mire. What a terror to face a "cruel" God (v. 21) and to feel that after being tossed about ruthlessly like a leaf before a storm, God will push him relentlessly into the house of death (vv. 22,23).

Job 30:24-31   The Unexpected Response   Job just cannot understand the treatment he has received. When he was strong he wept for the distressed and grieved for the poor. Yet there is no such sympathy or help for him. Verses 28-31 are amazing and devastatingly eloquent, "I go about blackened, but not by the sun; I stand up in the assembly, and cry for help. I am a brother of jackals, and a companion of ostriches."[2]

JOB'S OATH OF INTEGRITY/JOB 31

Job had previously challenged God to meet him and either present His case or let Job speak (Job 13:20-24). Now he plays out his role as the accused, even though there is no evidence that God is paying any attention to him. He will take his solemn oath, his hand on the Bible so to speak, and protest his innocence.

This is amazingly high ground. In some ways it seems an affirmative response to the kind of ethics Jesus advanced in the Sermon on the Mount. There is emphasis on thought and motivation as well as on actions. Job's claims are unsettling. Seventeen times Job will take an oath, effectively saying, "Not Guilty" to an impressive list of possible moral defections.

Job 31:1-12   Clearance from Deceit and Adultery   Job begins with awareness of his need of inner purity (vv. 1-4). He has made a covenant with his eyes, an internal commitment to abstain from lust because he knows that God sees his ways and that calamity would have to be the result of his disobedience.

His formal oath was a statement of the crime, which he repudiated by calling a curse down upon himself if he were guilty. This was a most solemn statement.

He first claims that he has been free of falsehood and deceit; his heart and his hands are pure (vv. 5-8).

He then claims moral purity. He has not coveted his neighbor's wife. Were he to be guilty, the same indignity should come to him. His wife should take the part of a slave and be ravished by others. This would have been the greatest possible humiliation to a husband of that time.

Job 31:13-23   Clearance from Abuse of Power   Job now denies guilt in relation to his use of power and wealth. He has not mistreated his servants, men or women. He has an amazingly advanced concept of the brotherhood of men in the sense that all men are creatures of God. Job would have no idea of man's equality, but he had a high view of responsibility.

He was rich and a master of men. Others were

poor and enslaved. Job has been a friend to the orphan, the widow, the poor and the powerless.

We have to be impressed with the high ideal of neighbor love that moved the tragic hero. It is a beautiful picture of social concern. Job felt it an affront to the majesty of God for him to eat his food alone when there might be an orphan going hungry.

Yet when Job speaks about the reason for his concern, it sounds amazingly like the theology that has been relentlessly applied by the friends. Job knew that if he did not do the right thing, calamity would descend upon him and he could not have faced the "majesty of God" (v. 23).

Job 31:24-34 Clearance from Impure Heart
Job now turns inward and considers his personal attitudes. He has not trusted his money, nor has he been enticed into a subtle or sophisticated idolatry. Notice that Job is not about to bow down to gross idols, nor to "cover all the bases" by just a glance of respect at the sun or an aesthetic kiss of the hand as a tribute to unseen powers (vv. 26,27). Regardless of the cultural setting, idols are always close at hand. Job is aware of a jealous God, who brooks no rivals, and he has not been false to his creator.

Job then declares that he has never found any pleasure in the ruin of those who hate him. This is high ground for the Old Testament, where love of enemy is virtually unknown, and where there are frequent expressions of imprecation, even fierce hatred. (See Psalms 58:10; 109:6 ff.) Certainly it is most unexpected for us to find a man who shows no exultation at the ruin of his enemy, for such ruin could be an act of divine judgment. Yet Job swears that he finds no joy in the demise of his opponents.

Job also protests his openness of life. He has been a gracious host to the wayfarer, and he has never kept in hiding some wrong doing that would bring the contempt of the crowd around him.

Job 31:35-37 Appeal for a Hearing This outburst from Job is surprising in that he has not finished his series of oaths. It is the grand finale, the climax of the words of Job. Job now hurls his defiance at God in the most open and brazen manner. He wants an indictment, written against him. What has he done wrong? If he could have such an accusation, he would bind it to him "as a crown," and approach God "like a prince."

A careful reading of this passage will make us see why the Whirlwind becomes a necessity and why God speaks to Job eventually as one who "darkens counsel by words without knowledge." Job has gone too far. Though he has properly challenged a rigid theology that sees all trouble as evidence of guilt, he replaces it with an equally rigid principle of salvation by merit. He has no consciousness of the need for grace, only a demand of reward for virtue. The oaths of clearance have been increasingly pompous.

We might tolerate statements like this by others on Job's behalf and consider it exaggerated but well-meaning. For Job to be commenting on himself seems vain and arrogant. Job has skewered himself on his own sword. Job has not cursed God, but he has done something far worse. He has made God unnecessary.

This is the sin of man, first sadly acted out in a

garden that became a wilderness. It is the sin of being a god for yourself, or making God in your own image. When a man feels he has done everything that is expected and commanded, he has no need for grace, forgiveness or understanding. Job wanted only one thing—vindication and recognition. The boils and ashes, the taunts and stabs, the darkness and silence have finally taken their toll.

Job 31:38-40   Post Script About the Land   Possibly the poet deliberately put Job's shocking words just before the end, rather than at the end of the speech in order to heighten dramatic tension. It seems odd to us, but it may well have been most acceptable to him. There is no evidence of any textual corruption.

Since Job is a man of the land, the concluding appeal is for recognition of his judicious use of its resource. The land has not cried out against him, nor has he abused those who have tilled and kept it. This has a familiar ring in the day when ecology and preservation of natural resources have become a vital issue.

Job considers caring for the land a moral concern, not just an economic one. Ecological concerns today are perhaps enthusiastic in reverse proportion to how much these concerns affect a person economically. Until that alters to some degree, we will continue to violate our resources rather than tend and preserve them.

"The words of Job are ended" (v. 40). He has gone out without a whimper. He not only maintains his righteousness; he glories in it. Job is correct in the principle that his trouble did not come because of his sin. But in his headlong rush for vindication he has lost his humility and awe. Although he has kept the Law, or so he thinks, he has lost his sense of harmony and fellowship with God.

10
enterprising Elihu

THE FOURTH FRIEND/JOB 32—37

These six chapters constitute a most interesting and provocative section of the book of Job. Upon first reading of the opening verses of chapter 32, it is only logical to ask the question already echoed by scholars since the days of the rabbis: How did Elihu get here?

You might presume, as some have, that Elihu's discourse was not written by the Joban poet. Differences in style and content have led some to this conclusion. You might also presume that it really doesn't matter too much who wrote it. In one sense you might be right.

Whether or not it was part of the book at the time of the original writing is really an academic question. The passage could be left out without radically altering the book. Yet this passage does have a significant contribution to make. This section was appropriately inserted here for a reason. Remember that Job is a religious book, poetically constructed around a historical sequence, and not an attempt to give a documentary report of specific speeches.

When we read Elihu, we'll discover several differences about this discourse. Elihu is introduced in a different fashion. More pedigree is given for him than for any other character. He disappears as mysteriously as he came. No mention of him is made anywhere else in the book. He proceeds with his arguments in a fashion that differs from the approach of the previous dialogue. He pays much more attention to what Job has said. He is interested in catching Job in his own arguments and reasoning with principles that have already been raised. He does not bother to wait for any reply from Job or any of the friends. A linguist who reads the book also discovers Aramaic influences that are not discernible in the other sections.

Elihu's approach to Job's problem was not dealt with by the friends. Elihu wants to deal more realistically with the specific objections which Job raised. He wants to put down the objections and discover some meaning in sorrow and trials beyond the simple dimension of judgment. Elihu recognizes that divine justice may manifest itself in various ways, especially as it operates in society. This project will become more clear as we look at the four speeches that Elihu made.

Elihu's First Speech/Job 32 and 33

This speech will serve to introduce Elihu and the two main problems Job has raised.

Job 32:1-5 Prose Introduction The main state-ment of this paragraph is "his anger burned." Since it is repeated four times in five verses, we should be im-pressed that Elihu was really upset. Elihu's youth is given as the reason for his refusal to speak earlier. Although the older friends have said that Job is wrong, they haven't really answered his questions. So Elihu will speak and settle the matter.

Job 32:6-22 Poetic Introduction This is a florid statement in which Elihu introduces himself and jus-tifies his speaking. It is the closest thing in the book to humor. Elihu has waited, assuming that an old man is a wise man (v. 7). But he is disappointed. "It is not the old that are wise, nor the aged that understand what is right"[2] (v. 9). So he will speak.

He has his point. Age is not a guarantee of wis-dom, and the folly of age is to presume that it is wise. The church is promised that the Holy Spirit will come in power upon young and old (Acts 2:17), so that dreams and visions are not the sole property of the elderly. Even Jesus accomplished his work as a comparatively young man. If wisdom is openness to truth and readiness to learn, then it would follow that age is more eager to learn from youth than vice versa, but this is unfortunately not the case. Fre-quently youth possess the wisdom of courage and the insight of innovation that has been lost by their elders.

Elihu has been disappointed at the inability of the friends to answer Job (vv. 11,12). Now he can re-strain himself no longer. Like wine fermenting in a new wineskin, he is ready to burst (vv. 18,19). None of this seems destined to gain attention from Job or his friends, but nothing dissuades or discourages Elihu.

Job 33:1-7   Full of Words   Elihu says he is full of words (Job 32:18), and this is a passage to prove it. He is still winding up getting ready to pitch the first ball, and it seems as if he will never throw it. He assures Job that since he (Elihu) is just a man, Job can discuss the matter and respond to him quite freely. However, he doesn't ever seem to stop for breath so that anyone else could possibly answer back.

Job 33:8-13   Elihu Denies Job's Main Ideas   Elihu quotes from Job's own statements. Here is a case in point. Verse 9, "I am pure without transgression," is a quote from a number of possible texts; 9:21, "I am guiltless"; 10:7, "I am indeed not guilty"; 16:17, "There is no violence in my hands." Verse 10, "He counts me as His enemy," is from 13:24, "Why dost thou . . . consider me Thine enemy?" Verse 11, "He puts my feet in the stocks; He watches all my paths,'" is a direct quote from 13:27.

Elihu frankly states that Job is wrong. He will attempt to show the reasoning behind this, but he wants to make the categorical statement first. Sometimes this is a necessary procedure. Jesus says the same thing to the Sadducees in Matthew 22:29. Situations of false teaching or misrepresentation of Christian truth are often so gross that the first reaction can only be, "You're wrong!" Elihu brushes Job's main ideas aside as a tissue of lies.

Job 33:14-33   Experience Disproves Job   Job has raised two objections. First, he is innocent and God is unjustly persecuting him. Second, God does not answer him in his need. Seeking to show these statements incorrect, Elihu handles them in reverse order.

Job has said God doesn't respond to his condition. "Two major experiences in my life disprove that," says Elihu. The first is the revelation of impending judgment through dreams. Elihu believes that God communicates directly with men to spare them from untimely death. Eliphaz also professed such direct revelation (Job 4:13-21).

The other means of warning about death that God uses is sickness and pain. Elihu regards this as "chastening" (v. 19) and suggests that God will send angelic help to assist the sinner on the road to repentance. The passage beginning at verse 23 is intriguing for the Christian reader: "If there is an angel as mediator for him, one out of a thousand, to remind a man what is right for him, then let him be gracious to him, and say, 'Deliver him from going down to the pit, I have found a ransom;' Let his flesh become fresher than in youth, Let him return to the days of his youthful vigor.'" A ransoming mediator who shouts the victory of deliverance sounds to us very much like the Lord Jesus Christ.

However, the passage describes an angel, or messenger, providing assistance in repentance, interpreting the message of God to this man, calling to God's attention the change of heart and then requesting restoration. The Pit is Sheol or death, and Elihu feels that God disciplines men to spare them and gives angelic help to understand the discipline.

Elihu believes that God will do this an indefinite number of times. "Behold, God does all these things, twice, three times, with a man"² (v. 29). As long as man repents, God forgives and restores.

Elihu's Second Speech/Job 34

Elihu now turns to Job's first objection that he is innocent and is therefore being unjustly treated (Job 34:5,6). He points out that the natural corollary of this is to assume that there is no profit in serving God (v. 9).

Job 34:1-9 A Declaration of Job's Error In a mocking mood, Elihu scoffs at Job's irreligious statement. Job "drinks up derision like water"³ (v. 7), and is taking counsel from wicked men.

Job 34:10-37 A Refutation of Job's Error Religious argument is curious and interesting. Everybody wins; at least, in their own eyes, no one loses. This chapter is a formidable statement about the justice of God. Elihu flat-footedly states that God does not pervert justice nor do wickedly (v. 12). Elihu now speaks just like the friends, though he thinks himself gloriously different. He states that it is wrong for Job to say something that does not agree with the orthodox statement of the way things are. That's the last thing we would have expected from Elihu, considering the buildup he gave us. It did not enter Elihu's brain to try to find out what Job really meant, or to question his own statements as to whether they did justice to God and to the situation.

I think it is important that we remind ourselves frequently that these debates by Job and the friends and Elihu have never once stumbled on the mysterious reality of the contest described in chapters 1 and 2; nor has anyone had the humility to suggest that there might be something he didn't know about the whole matter.

However, Elihu does show some degree of consideration for Job that is missing in the others. He does not attempt to embarrass Job by giving any details of Job's supposed immorality. He just wants Job to learn from his sorrow.

Elihu's Third Speech/Job 35

The author does not want any kind of reply from Job, so Elihu's words keep pouring out. He turns to the problem of the profit, or lack of it, in serving God.

Job 35:1-8 Job Again Refuted Elihu now sounds very much like Job's friends, yet there is an interesting difference. He rejects Job's statement that virtue has no reward. Elihu reminds Job that God is independent of Job's sin. The Almighty is not frustrated by man's disobedience (vv. 3-7). A man may feel the results of his own disobedience, but God is above the transgressions of men. Elihu does not say that God is unmoved by them. He simply reminds Job that God isn't going to be ruined by what man does.

Job 35:9-16 When Man Is Proud, His Cry Is Not Heard Elihu places the problem squarely in man's response to his oppression and trouble. Man's sin brings injustice and difficulty. In the midst of this man cries out for deliverance, but not with a sincere desire for God. An animal can cry out in pain, but man can look to God, "who gives songs in the night" (v. 10). If Job has not received help it has been because of an "empty cry" (v. 13).

There is poignant beauty in this. Sorrow ought to produce an aesthetic creativity that brings us to God. God can give "songs in the night." Something of the amazing power of music to lift the heart and penetrate the deepest crevices of the soul is hinted at in this word. I think immediately of that dynamic duo, Paul and Silas, who shook a prison with their praises at midnight, even though they were in chains. (See Acts 16:24,25.)

In a broader sense, this may also be saying that the capacity of art to transcend our human predicament is only discovered in the darkness of pain.

Elihu's Fourth Speech/Job 36 and 37

Elihu's concluding statement, the clearest evidence of the progress in thought he has made, contrasts with the static condition of his friends. This is not to deny the insufferable quality of Elihu's wisdom. We cannot avoid verse 4: "For truly my words are not false; One who is perfect in knowledge is with you."'

Job 36:1-25   Elihu's Explanation of God's Way with Man   Elihu gives for the last time his ideas on the divine methodology. God judges the incorrigible with death (v. 6), but even the righteous must be purged and instructed. Their affliction opens their ears to the teaching of God (v. 10) and when they listen and obey, God restores them to prosperity (v. 11). Several verses in this section are extremely difficult to translate (vv. 16,17,18).

Elihu comes close to the message that Job is shortly to receive from God. He calls Job to learn from his present affliction rather than bitterly reacting against it. Elihu is also concerned about Job's desire for Sheol, and warns him against such an attitude (vv. 20,21).

Job 36:26—37:24 God's Greatness in Nature Elihu closes with an impressive hymn to God's power revealed in nature. How amazingly is the Hebrew genius guided by the Holy Spirit in avoiding any sentimental or pantheistic view of nature. With pious consistency the Joban poet, as well as the Psalmist of Scripture, glorifies God through nature, but never nature itself. There is no expression for or sense of "Nature" in the Bible.

Elihu's hymn exalts God as the Lord of the seasons. He begins with autumn, the rainy season of the Near East, and he is especially awed by the crashing thunder (Job 36:26—37:5). Then comes winter, with snow, ice and the hibernating animals (Job 37:6-13). He concludes with a description of summer, and its scorching heat (Job 37:14-24).

All of this is an appropriate prelude to the Voice from the Whirlwind that will take up this theme and challenge Job to reply. Elihu has at least left Job with an awesome view of the majesty of God, even though he closes his discourse with one last slash at the sufferer, "He does not regard any who are wise in their own conceit"[2] (v. 24).

II

voice from the whirlwind

JOB'S ENCOUNTER WITH GOD

This extended debate must have an ending. Just about everything that might be surmised about this situation has been said, and we imagine a kind of dramatic pause, the silence of anticipation.

Then it happens. The only possible fitting conclusion for this epic poem—God speaks from the Whirlwind. This is a most unusual passage; indeed, it is unique in the Old Testament. The Word of the Lord is both a Mosaic and prophetic phenomenon. It is usually spoken through some person, in the white heat of inspiration, often in the form of an oracle, a judging or guiding word. But here, the longest passage purporting to be a divine utterance is obviously not the ecstatic or prophetic word, but the careful, majestic, magnificently executed, divinely inspired poetic masterpiece of the Joban poet. Both the dialogue and this passage come from the same pen, but this is unquestionably the greater work. It is a serious matter to write for God, and this author displays a profound awareness of that responsibility. One commentator of another generation observed: "This first speech of Jehovah transcends all other descriptions of the wonders of creation or the greatness of the Creator which are to be found in the Bible or elsewhere."

Job has insistently called for an intervention from God. (See Job 9:13-19; 10:5-22; 13:14-21.) To his amazement, he gets it. This is not a theophany, in that God never appears to Job or his friends. After the Whirlwind, Job finally admits that he has seen God, but it is not through vision in the normal or even religious sense. The Whirlwind links this revelation of God with the kind of event commonly spoken of in connection with the end of the world and its judgment. (See Isa. 29:6; 40:24; 41:16; Jer. 23:19; 30:23; Ezek. 1:4; Zech. 9:14.) Even the Hebrew word for the Whirlwind indicates final judgment and consummation.

Job is wonderfully ready for this divine Word. He has been rebuked by his friends for his attitude toward God, and properly so. Yet Job has not renounced God, even though he has expressed his frustration with Him. Disappointed and puzzled as he is, Job has nevertheless clung tenaciously to the God he knows. Nor has he regretted the integrity which he so staunchly defended against the attacks of his friends. It now seems to him that integrity doesn't make much difference in the way God treats a man, but still he isn't sorry that he feared God and turned away from evil.

Job and his friends have come to common ground. They all agree that Job has been cut off from God. Their only disagreement is about why this has happened. The problem we now face is how to restore Job and help him through to faith with integrity, and yet not reveal to him or to his friends the strange divine purpose behind this whole drama. He cannot know of the contest with the Satan to show that Job's sole motive for trusting God is love and devotion rather than a desire for the blessing God can give. If Job is told the story behind the story, all those who must suffer in the dark will never profit from his experience. It is important that they do profit. Suffering in the dark is really the only true suffering in the world.

Job has come to believe that there are areas of life over which God either has no control or takes no interest. So he must be convinced that God is sovereign, fully possessed of the power and the will to control His world.

God chooses to show Job that His mysterious power and design in the natural world is evidence of His sovereignty. This is not to say that there is a one-to-one equation between the natural world and the moral order that Job was having such problems with. Job's difficulty is essentially one of the spirit. If he can return to an attitude of faith and full confidence, inspired by an awareness of the *mysterium tremendum,* the awful majesty of God as seen in the natural world, then he will be able to accept his suffering in humility and patience.

Perhaps even deeper than the awareness of majesty will be the awareness that God is *there,* that He has been with Job in the dunghill just as He was with Job in his elegant home. Since Job concluded that he had been abandoned by God, all he needed for therapy and restoration was the assurance that God would take notice of him and meet him personally.

God's First Speech

Job 38:1-3   God's Challenge What terror! "Who is this that darkens counsel by words without knowledge? Now gird up your loins like a man, and I will ask you, and you instruct me!"[1]

There is no introduction, no inquiry as to how Job is getting along or concern for his feelings. Job is to be a man, not a maggot as Bildad suggested (Job 25:6) or a prince, as Job has suggested (Job 31:37, but a man—just what he *is* and what God wants him to be.

Job 38:4-38   Mysteries of Earth and Sky Instead of giving any answers at all to the issues that have been raised, God proceeds to ask Job a new series of questions They remind us of the song "Were You There?" as God repeatedly challenges Job to answer the most intricate and demanding questions. There is a strange irony in all this. God almost taunts Job with the most unexpected statements. "Tell Me, if you have understanding" (v. 4); "Since you know," (v. 5); "Tell Me, if you know all this" (v. 18); "You know, for you were born then, and the number of your days is great!"[1] (v. 21).

It is difficult to feel just what this approach is calculated to accomplish. Here is a man whose children are all dead, and who wrestles with the moral order of the universe, and God asks him to explain natural processes. What if he could? Would this answer the problem of pain for a man in the ashes?

Yet God is bringing Job to a renewed (because he supposedly knew it before his troubles began) realization of just what it means to be man in a universe created by God. Pride is the great problem of mankind, and so it has been ever since the Garden. Job may not be a maggot, but neither is he God. Until he can respond with a little more insight into the routine responsibilities of the Deity, he should be more reserved in his evaluation of how the more intricate matters should be managed.

Man still needs this reminder. God may not use the same items to strike awe and wonder into man's heart today, but this does not mean there are no mysteries left. How odd that man feels so proud to discover the amazing realities of the physical universe, almost assuming that he himself has placed all these marvels there! If anything is lacking in the advance of science and technology, it is humility. This is not to demean the intelligence of men or deny the benefits of learning, but it is an admission that our wisdom to bring about the blessings of a good life for all mankind has not kept pace with our technological accomplishments.

What a magnificent poem this really is! God nostalgically remembers the laying of earth's cornerstone, "when the morning stars sang together, and all the sons of God shouted for joy'" (v. 7). Where was Job when God set the bounds for the sea (vv. 8-11) or brought forth the dawn, which is pictured as a person who, rising from sleep, takes a cloak that has been used as a blanket and shakes it out (v. 13)?

107

Job is asked about the springs of the sea and the gates of death, supposedly in the heart of the earth (vv. 16,17). Does he know the place of light and dark, the treasures of snow and hail, the channels for the rain? Can he superintend the progress of the stars, or command the clouds, with their lightning and thunder (vv. 19-38)? Even though our knowledge of some of these phenomena may be much greater than Job's, the grandeur and mystery of this passage remains.

Job 38:39—39:30 Mysteries of Animal and Bird Life God turns to the animal creation and questions Job about matters that properly mystified the ancients. The feeding of lions and ravens (vv. 39-41), the birth and growth of the mountain goats (vv. 1-4), the habits of the wild asses (vv. 5-8), the wild ox (vv. 9-12), the ostrich (vv. 13-18), the horse (vv. 19-25), the hawk (vv. 26-30) are all matters that Job cannot possibly understand.

Of exceptional beauty and power is the portion describing the horse, especially as a beast of battle, in which role it was so convincing in the ancient world.

Job's First Reply
Job 40:3-5 Job's Answer to God's Challenge Job's response is inevitable. There is absolutely nothing for him to say, so he puts his hand over his mouth to silence any possible outcry.

God's Second Speech
Job 40:6-14 God Invites Job to Rule Once more the Voice from the Whirlwind charges Job to answer. But now, since Job has presumed to question

God's governance of the world, God suggests that Job take over. If God has not been putting down the wicked and exalting the righteous properly, it is time for Job to do it. There is profound significance here. "Will you really annul My judgment? Will you condemn Me that you may be justified?"[1] (v. 8).

Perhaps the core of the problem is that when man determines to justify his own way, he usually ends up condemning God's way. Yet even now God does not condemn Job, nor does he attempt to list his shortcomings, or even call attention to his pride. But the love of God is beginning to shine through this veil of irony. If only Job were God then perhaps he could be acknowledged as capable. "Then I will also confess to you, that your own right hand can save you"[1] (v. 14).

How powerfully this really speaks to the present human predicament! With high self-esteem men decide what kind of universe God should run. It seems such a simple thing for man to describe a "good" world, with peace and love and equality, and the things that make for creature comfort abounding everywhere. Yet we forget what the problem of human sin and disobedience has meant to God.

We forget what involvement in our suffering, what identification with our wretchedness, was necessary to bring about a meaning and reality for these lives of ours. We forget how totally incapable we were and are to do anything to change this. As Christians we are driven back to the cross of Jesus, to discover anew in that mystery of suffering and death, the divine answer to our pride and rebellion.

Job was trying to destroy God's freedom by de-

manding that God act like Job. God retains His freedom, His mystery and His sovereignty. In confronting Job with the true nothingness of man, God acts,
not like a man, but like God.

*Job 40:15-24; 41:1-34   The Description of Be-
hemoth, and Leviathan*   The divine irony now continues in an almost playful vein. "Behold now, Be-
hemoth" (v. 15). This creature is commonly considered the hippopotamus. What an odd thing for God
to make this creature and Leviathan, the crocodile
(Job 41:1), the climactic evidence of God's power
and mystery! There are two possible responses to
this phenomenon. One is to presume that they are
later additions by another writer, which I would reject. The other is to suggest that these are not just
river animals from Egypt, but mythological creatures. In later Hebrew thought it was said that these
animals were created by God on the fifth day of Creation and would provide food for the righteous of
messianic times.

The descriptions are rather difficult. For one thing,
they are not very accurate if they indeed refer to the
specific creatures. Even the poetry of this passage is
not quite so grand. It is hard to feel that there is just
a literal meaning intended here. Perhaps this is a
kind of divine fantasy, a deliberate tolerance of a
joke, yet one that defies the puny powers of man.
How bizarre and inexplainable such creatures really
are! Yet Job is frightened when a crocodile sneezes,
so how can he hope to face the crocodile's creator?
(See Job. 41:18.)

I am intrigued by the totally unexpected and free
shape of this divine response. With textbook descrip-

tion, God makes Job listen to His proud and playful recital of the habits and habitat of these strange beasts. Yet right in the midst of this zoology lesson is a significant word: "Who has given to Me that I should repay him? Whatever is under the whole heaven is Mine'" (Job 41:11).

It is not inappropriate to see in this the firm but gracious reminder that God is the Author of man's salvation. Paul quotes this verse in Romans 11:35, where he discusses salvation and mercy as God's free act in Christ.

I have often heard the attempt made to prove that God had no obligation to man. I'm sure this is technically and theologically correct. In fact, history shows God relating to man, not out of obligation, but out of love. After the fall of man, God didn't wait around trying to decide if or when to show love to His creation. As the hymnwriter has said so well, "He saw me plunged in deep distress and flew to my relief." There is no time lag in the love of God because God Himself *is* love. The important point is not a question of whether He had to do anything to help us, but rather the reality that He had to do everything to help us. And that is exactly what He has done in Christ. When no amount of human goodness, even human obedience, could merit His favor, he has taken the initiative in showing us His love.

If it takes boils and an ash heap to bring us to a full realization of that strange, powerful love of God, then so be it. For some of us the "Hound of Heaven" chases us relentlessly down the nights and days, often through deep agony, until we learn that His name is love. Someday the reasons will be clear.

111

Again we have the unexpected poetic device of anti-climax. Job 41:11 is a pivotal and important statement, but the Voice returns almost doggedly to the description of the crocodile. I will re-emphasize the unique, almost playful way in which God deals with Job's problem. Here is Job, "all over boils," and the lecture continues on the biological wonders of a large lizard. Yet we cannot say that there is no point to this, for Job finds it most meaningful, and effective.

In trying to figure out why he was suffering, Job tried to "understand" God. The Voice from the Whirlwind showed him the truth—that he was not able to understand God, and neither are we. We have never been told that we must understand God. Our command is to love God. It must be admitted that we are also told to love each other, yet I doubt that any of us professes really to understand each other. We even have trouble understanding ourselves. The strange humor of our existence is that life always stays just beyond our power to keep it in a tidy and orderly package.

So the Voice from the Whirlwind ceases, and we await the response of this sufferer to whom the living God has given so much time and attention.

Job's Final Words

Job 42:1-6   Job's Repentance   This is a magnificent response. First, Job acknowledges his stupidity in light of the power and wisdom of God. "I know that Thou canst do all things, and that no purpose of Thine can be thwarted'" (v. 2). In verse 3 Job rephrases the earlier statement of God, "Who is this that darkens my counsel by words without knowledge?'" (Job 38:2), and admits that he was talking way beyond himself. Perhaps we need this reminder as well, especially if we readily assume that we have a great deal of knowledge about God and His works. We must not forget that what we do not understand is greater than what we do understand.

Verse 4 seems to be another quotation from the Voice of God, "Hear, now, and I will speak; I will ask you, and you instruct Me."' Job is ready now to declare to God, but in an entirely different spirit.

He is now satisfied that his experience of God is adequate and convincing. "I have heard of Thee by the hearing of the ear; but now my eye sees Thee"' (v. 5). The metaphor is clear. Before, Job's knowledge of God was traditional, secondary. He had heard about God. Now he had confronted God for himself. This experience was not hearsay, a religious brew from past reality. It was warm as life, as real as today. It was to Job what conversion is to modern man. This was the great discovery of the Reformation and the powerful reality of the great awakenings. This is the simple witness of a once-blind sinner, "One thing I do know, that, whereas I was blind, now I see"' (John 9:25).

It seems surprising to find this gospel reality at the heart of this Old Testament book. Yet because religion has always had a way of getting between God and man, it has therefore needed this correcting word. How many have been raised in religious homes, processed through the rites of the church, inducted into membership, encouraged to participate in religious worship and consider themselves in

113

friendly relationship to God, but still have no personal awareness of divine reality or transforming faith? Perhaps, like Job, they have the problem of pride, a refusal to bow before the mystery and majesty of God. Perhaps their hypnotic indifference requires some smashing blow to jolt them into awareness of reality. Regardless of how that awareness comes, its effect is the same. No joy in all the world is like that of the liberated soul, who has found life in Christ. There is no substitute for that reality. Job had found it.

The resulting statement seems terribly self-effacing but it is not. "Therefore I despise myself, and repent in dust and ashes"[2] (v. 6). Do not think, however, that this is the cry of despair. It indicates an interior attitude and motivation. "I despise myself" is equivalent to "melting into nothingness." What a change in Job! No longer crying out for vindication, he is willing to receive no answers and to ask no further questions. He does not want explanations; he has found God. His own insignificance and powerlessness no longer threaten him. He has experienced God's love.

Repentance is the sign of hope. Job's surrender is not merely giving up his own righteousness. It is joyful acceptance of the righteousness of God.

It is most important to understand that God's concern for Job is itself the evidence of God's love. Even though God has not answered Job's questions, he has answered Job. There is no love without sharing, and the God who loves Job shares somehow in his suffering. The Christian knows that the ultimate mark of that sharing is the Cross. Self-abhorrence is our natural and genuine reluctance to accept grace, even though it is the greatest evidence of our profound need of grace. What a brief statement the poet gives to Job, and yet what volumes it speaks!

12

epilogue of Job

In a brief passage that returns to the prose style of the Prologue, the Joban poet brings this great drama to a conclusion. We earlier noted that this part, along with the Prologue (ch. 1 and 2), is probably the traditional story of Job, yet this closing section is not unrelated to the Dialogue. We will look at the content and then discuss the very exciting and interesting reasons for this kind of finish for the story.

God and Job's Friends

Job 42:7-9   God Deals with Job's Friends   The first action is to set the record straight with the three counselors. Eliphaz receives the word from God for all three, that he and his companions are condemned for their poor theology. The sacrifice suggested is unusually large. The price for their mistake was high!

Along with the sacrifice is the instruction to get Job to pray for them. This Old Testament incident has been wrongly used to presume that God accepts the prayers of some more readily than others and that it is to our advantage to get particularly holy people to pray for us. This is to forget our present privilege to pray in the name of Jesus. There can be no better access or more powerful mediator for us than He.

It is interesting to note that this whole episode presupposes the events of the Dialogue and would be meaningless without it.

Reconstruction

Job 42:10-17   The Restored Prosperity of Job
It was no small matter for Job to obey God and pray for these friends who had added so much to his grief. Yet he does, and gains a reputation that has been somewhat overlooked. Ezekiel 14:14 ff., speaks of Job, along with Noah and Daniel, as a righteous intercessor.

Verse 10 uses the interesting expression "restored the fortunes of Job."' Some have said this is a subtle indication that the writing is after the Babylonian Captivity, although it is not impossible that the phrase developed earlier.

Job's relatives and friends appear. We have had no previous information about them, but they seem unembarrassed to rally to Job after his ordeal has finished. The gifts that they gave were symbolic of their sympathy and concern. Giving such gifts, even to those who already have much, is almost a universal custom.

Job's former possessions are doubled. This very deliberate statement shows that the doubling of his wealth was not accidental. God had restored his possessions and more. The thirteenth verse, which tells us he again had seven sons and three daughters, may well be a beautiful affirmation of the fact that he has not really lost forever the ones who died. Since he will see them again in heaven, there is no reason for a doubled number now. However, the word for seven is a difficult one here, and there is an ancient Jewish commentary that takes this word to mean fourteen, so that the number of his sons was doubled after all! The patriarchal society would see no point in doubling the number of daughters! But at least these were the fairest girls in all the land. Not only are their names given, but they are granted an inheritance with their brothers, another testimony to Job's generous and gracious spirit. This kind of regard for women is a frequent event in Old Testament history.

There is probably something missing from the text of verse 16. Only three generations are mentioned but it is described as four. By any standard Job certainly lived to a ripe old age.

So What?

We miss the point, however, if we are willing to let this brief narrative close our story without raising some more fundamental issues. This ending needs an explanation. The problem is that the conclusion actually refutes the whole point of the book—the fallacy of retributive justice. Job has been arguing for the idea that to obey God and live right does not guarantee prosperity. Job's friends have said that it does.

After it is stated that the friends are wrong, a repentant Job receives twice what he had before. That does sound as though righteousness pays. What is being taught?

There are several possible explanations. Some have concluded that the tradition of Job's restoration was so strong that the Joban poet could do nothing but fit his dialogue into it, even though it did not really serve his purpose. This is weak and unnecessary.

There is also the suggestion that this restoration serves as another act of grace, the evidence that though life does not proceed on a neat set of rules, yet there is an unexpected element of reward in life, just as there is an unexpected occurrence of trouble. Righteousness doesn't have to pay, but it may very well do so, and the best attitude of life is one that expects such rewards without actually demanding it. This is to say that the good man is more likely to experience the "happy ending," but that there could be situations where he wouldn't.

A less commendable suggestion just assumes that if Job is to be vindicated, it can only be in terms of success and prosperity. That is the only language the world can understand, so the story uses it. Yet this hardly seems within the spirit of divine freedom that the poet so magnificently reflects. Neither is there anything in the Epilogue that indicates the restoration of Job as a vindication for him, though that may well be implied.

There are two other considerations that I feel are far more appealing as explanations of this conclusion to the book. Let's remember what the whole story is about. God has thrown down a challenge to the Satan's contention that Job is serving God only because of the blessings that come from it. The trial has been set up and the prediction that Job will curse God to his face has proved untrue. Job has survived, not without great problem and painful growth. But he has survived, and the trial must now be concluded. Even then it will not be revealed to Job that there was a mysterious cosmic struggle behind his suffering.

But if his trial is to be concluded, there must be a return to the *status quo,* to something that duplicates the condition that prevailed when this all began. Job has been tried and he has been acquitted. It would seem unnecessary and unfair not to restore him. To be sure, a bonus is granted in the doubling of his possessions, but this is relative. He might have so increased in wealth anyhow, had not the trial been launched. The point is that he became again a prosperous man with a happy family. This is as good and straightforward an explanation as one could ask.

Yet there is a second possible explanation that penetrates even deeper and speaks more meaningfully to our condition. What does this restoration mean to Job personally? He has not received any answers to his questions or explanations for his sufferings. He is not informed that the contest is over and that he has won. God hasn't given any new guarantees of life.

Yet he takes life back again, a life which he was for a while rejecting and hating. What good does it really do to get back sheep and oxen? Job knows how quickly they can be taken away. What is there to prove it will not happen again? Above all there's that family of his, with all the risks of loving and caring. Who knows what might happen to them? Certainly Job remembers how the status quo suddenly became such a hollow mockery.

Yet Job knows something in a new way that he did not know before, something that makes this restoration possible and acceptable. He knows that God is concerned about him, and this concern can only mean that God loves him. Love has not conquered all, but love does affirm the meaning and beauty of existence. Love says that the risk is worth it, and that Job can take back his life, take back his responsibilities, take back his wife, his children, his friends, everything that has already proved so fragile and inadequate. It is the same for us. The love of God makes existence acceptable, even though we are not guaranteed immunity from disappointment or even tragedy.

This is one of the great words of this book, perhaps the great word. It is more than a simple explanation of suffering or a proof of God's justice in his ways with men. It is the key to life itself. It is the willingness to leave in unknown councils of the cosmos the determination of struggles and conflicts of powers that are beyond us. Paul was aware of this in speaking of the "principalities and powers" in the heavenly places. We may not know, indeed we cannot know, such mysteries, but we can see with the vision of faith the God whose power is still but faintly grasped.

13
summary

Does all of this say anything to the circumstances that you and I face in our daily lives? Unmistakably! When we began the study of this book we commented that this may well be the most practical of all the books of the Old Testament.

At the risk of being redundant, but in the interest of clarity, let me identify again the major mountains of truth that have emerged in this amazing landscape.

MOTIVATION

The first is the great principle and problem of motivation in serving God. "Does Job fear God for naught?" was the question of the Satan, and the development of the entire story is a test of that suspicion. Like any great question of life, this issue does not have a simple answer.

Let me rephrase the question, "Will a man serve

God when it seems that serving God doesn't pay?" It couldn't pay, at least for a while, for the test of Job to mean anything. Up to that time, the wise men, including Job, had worked out the reasonably reliable philosophy of life that you got out of life what you put into it; that the good man saw the results of his goodness, and the evil man reaped bitterness and calamity as due reward of his deeds. Job's trial pulled the rug out from under that whole position. It can never be the same again. In the crucible of affliction Job discovered that he could trust God and keep his faith. All he needed was to know God was there, not what God was doing, or why.

This does not remove the *ultimate* sense in which it *must* pay to serve God. It is better to serve God than not to serve Him, but that is a statement of faith, not of demonstrable fact. In Job's case the test was ended, the vindication came and the blessing was restored. This "test" of trusting is still going on for every Christian. We are committed to the service of Christ and counting on the certainty of His promises. We have no guarantee of any earthly gain or reward as a result of this service. We even are promised a large measure of difficulty and persecution for the simple reason that we are the followers of Jesus. (See Matt. 5:13-16.) We are servants, He is the Master, and we cannot expect "rewards" from life that He did not receive. But we are still convinced that it "pays" to serve Jesus, in that all the trials and problems of this world will pale into nothingness in the light of the glory of God promised to His own. (See 2 Cor. 4:17,18.)

Job's story teaches us that it is foolish to seek to

determine why the world has to be this way, or more especially, why particular things may happen to us. This is not to be confused with a resigned attitude of passive acceptance. The dynamic of faith wrestles with hostile powers and fights against the wrong within and without. We are not to be those who cringe in the corners of life, comforting our empty stomachs with the promise of pie-in-the-sky-by-and-by.

What God asked of Job was to live "as though." He was to live in paradox, as though it was eminently worthwhile to serve God when for the moment it was not working out that way at all. The only way that Job finally found strength to live "as though" was in confrontation with God in the Whirlwind, the God of Hope, the God of Final Destiny. That is really what is being asked of us today.

We are living "as though" the final victory of Christ had already taken place. Indeed, the assurance and evidence of that victory has been given to us in the resurrection of Jesus from the dead. I hope you see that I am not defining our faith in God as something that is of such pure motivation that it makes no difference what happens to us. I cannot honestly say that I would still love God, if it *never* brought good to me. Even Job could not stand being suspended in the vacuum of meaninglessness. It was not that he got the answer, but he got the God who is the answer. We ask the same, and in Christ we receive it. Then we can live "as though" citizens of the Kingdom of God.

There should be a warning with this understanding of the enigma and mystery of the sufferings of the righteous. We must guard against saying that there is no connection between what we do and what happens to us. Some things that happen to us, both good and bad, may be undeserved. But many more things are, in fact, the direct result of our choices and actions. We are now what we have been becoming, and life will continue to have that dimension of cause and effect, judgment and reward. Again we are forced to an awareness of the ultimate. There just isn't room in the narrow confines of human life to play out all the implications of what we do or don't do.

The bad man does not consistently receive the "due reward" of his deeds. But Paul's statement, "Be not deceived; God is not mocked: for whatsoever a man soweth, that shall he also reap" (Gal. 6:7), is still solemn truth for present existence. There is also truth in the present joy of serving God. "These things I have spoken to you . . . that your joy may be full,"[2] said Jesus (John 15:11). It is wrong for us to paint a dismal picture of the Christian life. Serving God brings more smiles than tears, but it is the tears that test us, and it is in the valley of sorrow that we need the understanding that the book of Job so marvelously brings.

CONFRONTATION WITH GOD

Without imposing New Testament understanding on an Old Testament experience, I choose the significance of Job's confrontation with God as the second great peak of spiritual reality seen in this book. Job considered his encounter with the Word of the Whirlwind to be the moment above all others: "Now my eye sees Thee"[1] (Job 42:5).

This is the great climax of the awesome story of a man who, all would presume, knew God as well as anyone could have known Him. There could hardly be a better model. Everything about him seemed to proclaim that he was on the inside when it came to religious matters. At first he even survived, with stoic fortitude and pious platitude, the loss of virtually everything a man could lose and still be alive. Yet here the formulas failed and God himself had to address Job.

It was not enough to have an orthodox theology. It was not enough to have been generous and just. It was not enough to have been an excellent father and a model citizen. It was not enough to have the advice and counsel of well-meaning and intelligent friends. Nothing less than God could meet Job's need, and nothing less than God was the Speaker from the Whirlwind.

God is always and inevitably just there, at the end of our rope. It is not that we know nothing of God elsewhere, but when we are in a storm, we will listen to God. The knowledge that is most truly personal comes when we realize ourselves stripped of all pretense and pride, with no answers and tons of questions, and a packful of good deeds that have turned to ashes. It is then that we realize our own presumption, our defiant demands for the universe to make sense to us, our calling God to account as to why He doesn't do things the way we so clearly see they should be done. He has to hold His mirror to our shouting and often peevish face, and remind us that He is there and that He has not abdicated the throne of His universe and that He knows us by name.

Though the book of Job does not actually say much about the love of God, it is but a brief step from the Voice of the Whirlwind to the Cry from the Cross. Neither gives the answer to why we seem forsaken, but both tell us that God is in the midst of the problem and has somehow made it His own. In His acceptance we can accept ourselves, our humanity, our frailty and our ignorance—and the Whirlwind becomes a great Calm.

REDEEMER/RESURRECTION

The third contribution of Job is in reality a twin peak: the call for the Redeemer and the hope of resurrection. These amazing ideas are very much woven together. We remember the three figures under which Job sees this very-needed person. The first is in 9:33, "There is no umpire between us, who might lay his hand upon us both."[2] Job was in a defiant mood, confident in his integrity, but hopelessly outweighed. His hope is in someone who could properly relate to God and man, a mediator who would ideally be both God and man, "the man Christ Jesus."

The second figure is in chapter 16. Job has despaired of any hope for vindication, but dares to believe that his case will not be closed until his "witness" for the defense appears. "Even now, behold, my witness is in heaven, and my advocate is on high"[1] (Job 16:19). There is no real fulfillment of this hope other than in Jesus, whom Paul described as, "at the right hand of God, who also intercedes for us"[1] (Rom. 8:34).

The third figure is in chapter 19, and here Job identifies this "man for others" as the *go'el,* the Re-

128

deemer. "And as for me, I know that my Redeemer lives, and at last He will take His stand on the earth'" (Job 19:25). Again Job speaks more than he knows. There will be one who can deliver the oppressed from captivity and lift the yoke of slavery. Again it is Jesus, "in whom we have redemption through His blood, the forgiveness of sins'" (Eph. 1:7).

In this last passage we find so vividly the anticipation that this Redeemer will be part of a great event that includes the resurrection of Job to new life (Job 19:26). Job seems to believe that in his flesh he shall see God. For him this idea has been difficult in coming. He toyed with it in chapter 14, but had to finally conclude that there was just no way for him to hope for this. Yet the shadowy concepts of Sheol were just not enough.

Job's thought was probably a significant factor in the development of the doctrine of resurrection in the Old Testament. By the time of Jesus it was a point of vigorous debate between the Pharisees and the Sadducees. The importance and significance of the doctrine is shown in the great foundation-truth of the gospel, the resurrection of Jesus. There is much more to this than interesting religious history. This is the very stuff of life itself. Job believed in a Redeemer through whom he would live anew and see God.

Job is long since dead, but what of his faith? You too are part of a great, presently living human family but you are equally mortal. All of your friends and dear ones will ultimately be taken from you, and then you, yourself, will face the reality of death. Nothing can avert this.

We foolishly build our security on the slippery

sands of possessions, or assume that our name perpetuated in the life and work of those who follow us will give us comfort and peace. We join the mass of people who lull themselves into apathetic indifference with the subtle drugs of entertainment or involvement that silence our deepest concerns. But Job was right at the bedrock of existence, and the hope of resurrection was affirmed to him by a confronting and imposing God. Although we may not muse from the ash heap after losing everything we ever had, that same God is the source of our hope as well.

background to the book of Job

AUTHORSHIP AND DATE

That Job was a person of great godliness and well-known in Jewish history seems apparent from the references in Ezekiel 14:14,20. But no one knows for sure who actually wrote the book. Since we can hardly expect Job to compose magnificent poetry while sitting on an ash heap, and since he couldn't have recorded his own death (see Job 42:17), we can safely conclude that the author was not Job himself. It is enough that Job was a good and righteous man. We don't have to make him a literary genius as well.

Many authorities believe the book was written by an unknown poet who appears to have been a deeply religious person of wide-ranging and perceptive intellect. This "Joban poet's" explanation of the most profound truth about God and man, under the guidance of the Holy Spirit, produced a volume that commands the respect of the ages.

Others have concluded that the contents of Job were written by more than one person. Different positions seem to carry the marks of different authors, especially the Prologue and Epilogue, in contrast to the poetic Dialogue. Whereas the Prologue-Epilogue reflects the basic story, certain modifications could have been made by the poet to relate the story to his major work, the Dialogue. Older traditions may have included additional statements by the friends concerning Job and his condition, perhaps in the same vein as his wife's encouragement to blaspheme God.

Some may have problems at this point in feeling that any of these explanations about the author destroy the "historical validity" of the book. I would not for a moment question the historicity of Job and the divine authority of the book to teach us about God, Satan, man, sin, suffering, etc. There is no reason to deny that a man named Job actually experienced what is described in this book. Nor do we do the book any harm by seeing it as the inspired work of an author who lived long after Job and used the story as the framework on which to hang this great fabric of poetic teaching.

The Christian need never be preoccupied with the human authorship to the exclusion of the great fact of divine authorship. As Peter tells us, holy men of old were "moved by the Holy Spirit'" (2 Pet. 1:21). No matter who wrote Job, it is still the Word of God and it speaks to us today.

Ambiguity about the author brings with it ambiguity about when the book was written. Early Christian writers dated the book quite early, even before Moses. Some consider it the oldest book in the Bible because the general conditions are similar to patriarchal times, and because it makes no mention of the Mosaic Law or any ordinances of the Tabernacle or

Temple. Others see it as written as late as the seventh century B.C. just before the exile of Judah. They say the theology of Job is more developed than that of patriarchal times. While the debate goes on, the date Job was written remains as uncertain as ever.

TEXTS AND TRANSLATIONS

Some passages in Job almost defy translation. If you have a study Bible with any marginal notes at all, you will see that Job takes the prize for alternative readings! But the man of faith need not be alarmed. Admitting that there are many problems with the text of the book of Job is not a lack of faith. It is not a tragedy to be indefinite about a verse that is understandable either way it may read. As in the rest of Scripture, the variations in problem passages do not affect the great truths of our faith, but they should serve to keep any teacher or commentator humble.

Because of the many problems in the original Hebrew text, it is difficult to select one translation which is better than all the others. The poetic majesty of Job is in some ways best preserved in the mighty cadences of the *King James Version*. And although that translation is sometimes obscure, many will always look to it as the finest expression of the language of Job.

Yet the aim of the Christian student should be to know accurately what the Bible says as well as to feel its literary power. At what point either of these elements should be compromised is a problem for the individual. For accuracy of text (as far as this is possible), the *New American Standard Bible* is not surpassed. For correction of the *Authorized Version* with more advanced textual readings but a sincere attempt to keep the poetic expression of that early work, the *Revised Standard Version* will appeal to many. Perhaps the best version is the read one, regardless of the description on the title page.

WISDOM LITERATURE

The book of Job is part of a definite class of Old Testament writings, known as "Wisdom Literature," which includes Job, Proverbs, Ecclesiastes and many of the Psalms. Wisdom Literature is part of the writings, the third general division of the Hebrew Bible, the other two being the Law and the Prophets (cf. Luke 24:44). As the name "Wisdom" implies, this kind of writing concentrates on practical and experiential truth gleaned from divinely inspired common sense. When we read through these books, a number of characteristics emerge:

1. The subject matter is derived from the practical demands of daily living. It proceeds to apply truth about God to these demands, rather than starting with religious truths and leaving the reader to figure out how they apply to life. The collectors of wisdom are not dramatic orators, but kindly and observant fathers, with deep concern to transmit a common sense that preserves a God-fearing, practical piety.

2. Another mark of Wisdom Literature is its universal character. It is the most "non-Israelitish" part of the Old Testament. The action in Job takes place in foreign territory. There is no mention of the Mosaic Law or the priesthood, and nothing of national history.

3. The generous use of nature as an illustration of the subject is also a characteristic of these books. This gives the material a universal quality, a home-spun familiarity that speaks to the human condition from figures that are common.

4. The very nature of this literature makes possible many sources, many authors. This is not in any sense to detract from the work of the Holy Spirit, who in various times and in various ways spoke to the fathers (see Heb. 1:1).

POETRY

The major portion (Job 3—41) of the book is poetry. The art of song or poetry was really a part of the larger classification of Wisdom Literature, since the poet or musician was vitally involved in all phases of Jewish life. There is virtually no distinction between wisdom and song in Jewish thought.

The basic characteristic of Hebrew poetry is its parallelism, that is, the artful repetition of a thought so as to reinforce and enhance it. The poet gives his idea synonymously by saying the same thing in a slightly modified way. A careful look at almost any passage in Job, Psalms or Proverbs will demonstrate this method. Consider Job 6:8-9.

"O that I might have my request,
  and that God would grant my desire;
that it would please God to crush me,
    that he would let loose his hand and
    cut me off!"[2]

Poetry is the language of art. It moves in figures, in symbols, in the kind of speech that says most when it is allowed freedom to be non-literal, non-technical.

This does not for a moment destroy the literal truth that is being taught or suggested. Nor does it mean that Job's experiences were not historical.

coordinated reading schedule

Read the parallel assignments from the book of Job and from this book *before* each class session. Notice that the assignment does not always include the entire chapter in *Why Me, God?* Sometimes you will read only those sections of the chapter designated by the subheadings.

for further reading

Blackwood, Andrew, Jr. *A Devotional Introduction to Job.* Grand Rapids: Baker Book House, 1959.

Davidson, Francis, ed. *The New Bible Commentary.* London: Inter-Varsity Fellowship, 1953.

Dhorme, E. *A Commentary on the Book of Job.* Camden, N.J.: Thomas Nelson, Inc., 1967.

Ellison, H. L. *A Study of Job.* Grand Rapids: Zondervan Publishing House, 1958.

Johnson, L. D. *Out of the Whirlwind.* Nashville: Broadman Press, 1971.

Pope, Marvin. *The Anchor Bible,* "Job". New York: Doubleday and Co., Inc., 1965.

Rowley, H. H. *The Century Bible,* "Job". Camden, N.J.: Thomas Nelson, Inc., 1970.

Terrien, Samuel. *Job: Poet of Existence.* Indianapolis: Bobbs-Merrill Co., 1957.

The superior numbers with Scripture quotations throughout this book refer to the following Bible versions.

1. *New American Standard Bible* © The Lockman Foundation, 1971. Used by permission.

2. *Revised Standard Version,* copyrighted 1946 and 1952 by the Division of Christian Education of the NCCC, U.S.A., and used by permission.

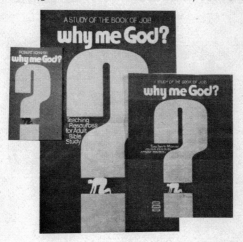

THE LOVE LIFE

Donald Grey Barnhouse

Compiled from the notes and sermons of the late Dr. Donald Grey Barnhouse, a Bible expositor famous for his vivid illustrations and challenging call to discipleship, the student Regal text presents an incisive, provocative commentary on key passages of John.

Study resources include a teaching manual with teaching plans and background information; discussion starters and numerous learning activities.

COMPLETE RESOURCE KIT

AVAILABLE FROM YOUR REGULAR CHURCH SUPPLIER

G/L REGAL BOOKS

A BIBLE COMMENTARY FOR LAYMEN (26 sessions)